MW01232681

IN THE

Valley of Achor

To Susan,
Much love, many
blessings!
PB

By Patricia Gaddis Brandon

xulon PRESS

Table of Contents

Introduction

I was first diagnosed with transverse myelitis, which is an inflammatory disorder of the spinal cord. Later, at Johns Hopkins Hospital in Baltimore, Maryland, that diagnosis was changed to vascular myelopathy, or a mechanical malfunction in the spinal cord blood supply system. Since both of these conditions are rare, and present with similar features, they are easily confused, or misdiagnosed. In my case, it is believed that long-term, repeated lifting of my garage doors, and the subsequent, hyperextension of my back, along with other unknown, possibly genetic, factors, contributed to this rare type of paraplegia. Similar to a phenomenon known as "surfer's stroke," in which first-time surfers experience the same initial symptoms that I did, it is believed that a blood vessel in my spine became kinked, like a garden hose; thereby temporarily depriving my spinal cord of vital oxygen for a period of time. In this respect, the effect is that of a stroke, and is therefore often referred to as a "mini-stroke of the spinal cord". As of the initial stages of the writing of this book, I am confined to a wheelchair, and paralyzed from the hips down, with many of the ensuing complications.

The title of this book is taken from two specific biblical references to the Valley of Achor. Joshua 7:10-26 tells the story of Achan, an Israelite who fought with Joshua in the battle for Jericho. Against the command of God, Achan steals from the spoils of war and brings divine displeasure upon Israel. For his sin, he is stoned in the Valley of Achor, rendering it a place of sadness and isolation. But, also in reference to Israel, Hosea 2:14-15 reads, "Therefore I am now going to allure her; I will lead her into the wilderness and speak tenderly to her. There, I will give her back her vineyards, and will make The Valley of Achor a door of hope. There, she will sing as in the days of her youth, as in the day she came out of Egypt." The Hebrew word for extreme trouble or affliction is "achor". In the Joshua account, the Valley of Achor is associated with deep trouble or sin and separation from God. Then, in the Hosea passage, in the midst of sin, trial and desolation, the Almighty speaks mercy and renewal to Israel; thus, returning her to her prior joyful relationship with God. The Valley of Achor, once a wilderness of sadness, becomes a "door of hope"!

Wilderness can be experienced as both lonely and frightening, as well as invigorating and a place of unparalleled beauty and renewal. Even Christ was led into the rugged wilderness to pray; to draw strength from the nearness of God, cut off from worldly comforts and distractions. The theme of the Hosea passage, like so many in the Bible, is one of redemption. No matter what devastating wilderness valley experience we may be facing in our lives, God "speaks tenderly" to us, opens a "door of hope", and invites us to "sing, as in the days of youth" and "return to our vineyards".

I fell in love with the Hosea passage because of the feminine reference to Israel, and other parallels to my own life. As a lover of both singing and wine, I often picture myself sitting in my wheelchair, miraculously coming to my feet, and literally jumping for joy – singing, and with wine in hand, and bounding through that open door of hope, as I return to a former physical state, but perhaps a greatly enhanced spiritual one, as well. I know that my own "achor" experience will be lengthy and difficult, at best –going from sad wilderness to singing in the vineyard. Truthfully, I am not sure what the worst part could be, or what any kind of recovery might look like. But I have come to know that God promises He will not leave, and that – somehow, some way – I will not only be ok, but my life will be greatly enriched, if I am willing to walk through that door of hope. And that – exactly that! – is my continued daily prayer.

Many have had, and will have, an extreme "achor" experience, from Moses, to Elijah, to John the Revelator, to Christ in Nazareth, in the wilderness of Judea. However, these experiences are not limited to people of Biblical times. Corrie ten Boom, the Dutch Christian woman whose family was imprisoned for helping Jews escape the

Nazi Holocaust, went on to bring many to Christ, through her own suffering. Nelson Mandela was imprisoned for years, prior to becoming President of South Africa. Does God cause these difficult, sometimes terrifying, tragedies – the "extreme achors"–to happen? Are they the result of God testing or teaching us, or are they perhaps the product of sin in this world? Could they be the result of our own poor choices, or those of others? I am neither a theologian, nor a student of Biblical hermeneutics, so I will humbly leave that discussion to those more knowledgeable on such matters.

The fact is, unfathomably terrible events happen in the world in which we live, and we do not have complete understanding of why or how long to endure. Matthew 5:45 tells us that, *"He causes his sun to rise on the evil and the good, and sends rain on the righteous and the unrighteous"*. The paradox is that life is both beautiful and brutal. It was for Christ, and it is so for us. What I do know is that God loves us, His children, and wants to work for good in our lives, no matter the circumstances. He understands human pain and suffering–His

Son lived it! This theme is repeated, many times, throughout the Bible. While we are never promised care-free, painless living, we are promised that God will never leave us; that He loves us, especially in the midst of the darkest, deepest valleys. He wants to be loved by us, as well. When we give our praise and faith, especially in times of distress and deep loss, He will work for the good, always.

This book is a reflection of my own "achor" experience; more specifically, of my faith journey, in the wake of sudden and frightening paralysis that occurred in the midst of a very active and satisfying life. Physicians at Johns Hopkins perhaps expressed it best when they stated that, while they could not guarantee that I would ever walk again, they could find no reason why I could not, with much hard work, and perseverance. I found it rather refreshing that highly esteemed physicians would comfortably acknowledge that some healing is beyond even their amazing skills. And so I wait in my own valley, remaining in a delicate balance between learning to navigate and embrace life with a physical disability, while vowing not to give up the fight to walk again. I do not know if I will physically recover completely, or no. Perhaps I should say that I do not know the timing of God in granting my request. Though the gift of walking is my continued prayer, I do know that, in the end, all will be made whole again, in God's way, in His perfect grace and time. Mine is a journey that seems to be taking a step forward, a few backward, then forward once again. Puns intended! Slow progress, as is the healing. You get the idea. I tried to give a real and honest account of this journey, thus far, and at times, I am certain that my guardian angel is lying prostrate on the floor, engaged in a measure of celestial head-banging of sorts. Thank goodness, we have a merciful God who understands our humanity! So, I give thanks daily – and yes, it is trying on some days–for specific blessings, both large and small, and for His help in fighting fear and worry about that which I cannot control. Patience, perseverance, and hope – always hope – are virtues I seek each day on this long journey.

Dedication

To my daughters, McKenna and Gracyn, the greatest blessings in my life: I love you more than you will ever know.

To Henry Gaddis, one tough soldier: Capta Majora, Dad!

To Mildred Causey, who was the finest English teacher and cherished friend: Here is that book you always wanted me to autograph. Thank you for believing I could.

Acknowledgements

To my extended family: Thank you for all of your love and support!

To the members of my St. Michael and All Angels Episcopal Church family: Thank you for being Christ to me.

To the "Rockbridge Fire Department and Demolition and Bathroom Remodeling Crew"– who asked for anonymity, but you know who you are – the mess, blood, sweat, tears, cold beer, wings, and laughter got me through the early days at home and made my predicament more bearable–and definitely cleaner.

To nurse tech Debra, who was a light in the darkness. I will never forget you.

To my friends: Thank you so much for the endless cards, letters, flowers, food, gifts, massages, and visits. How blessed I am to have you. Special thanks to Julie Wilson, who made sure I got to the early days of physical therapy and much more on a regular basis; and to Alicia Beam, who handles "big grocery store runs" with finesse, and also got me to physical therapy.

To all of the medical staff that demonstrated compassionate care on my behalf; especially Johns Hopkins Drs. Pardo and Gailloud; The Health South Rehab Facility Staff, especially Jill Polhemus; The Muscle Development Center/SC Department of Vocational Rehabilitation Staff, especially Barbara Jolly and Ella Dunham. What amazing work you all do!

To Kat Languell, who literally got me to work, helped make my deck an oasis of beauty, and is a constant friend.

To my clients, who honored me with entrance into their world; thus, allowing escape from my own chaos, and reminding me of the importance of helping others, always.

In The Valley, Part One

Isaiah 41: 13 "For I am the Lord, your God who takes hold of your right hand and says to you, Do not fear; I will help you."

June 28, 2014 5:30 A.M.

*L*ying in bed, I couldn't help but smile as I glanced at my cell phone to check the time. Wouldn't you know I'd be wide awake on a Saturday way before I had to be? I actually love this placid time of morning, so I didn't really mind. Outside was a lush, dark grayish hue, not yet a glimmer of the rising sun that would heat up another southern summer scorcher. Annie, our 15-yr old black lab, terrified of the slightest hint of inclement weather, had slept on the floor at the foot of my bed, after a few flashes of lightening the evening before. Now, she was rooting around the room, doing all she could to make her presence known. May as well get up, make a quick bathroom stop, let her out, and jumpstart the day. With errands to run for a much-anticipated virgin voyage to Europe–only three days away, now–it was going to be a packed Saturday. Maybe I could grab coffee and have my morning devotional out on the deck before I get started on all that needed to be done. I couldn't help but smile with excitement. I was so ready to begin this adventure. It seemed I'd waited all my life to finally get to Europe.

Pondering briefly on my many blessings, I laid quietly for a moment. How fortunate to not only have early retirement from school counseling these past three years, but to also be able to practice part-time at a local outpatient counseling center, still doing what I love on my own time, and to be actively involved in community mediation, and a host of other activities. Being single at this stage in my life, and able to take little excursions to the mountains, the beach, or to see my wonderful daughters, each only an hour away, or just being able to play my guitar, play tennis, spend time with many friends, and to visit with my aging father daily, were more than enough blessings. And to be able to drive my "fun car" – a 1990 red Miata convertible–on comfortable mornings such as this, made my world that much better. To think that two weeks ago I had been to a music festival in North Carolina, and then to our annual family beach gathering just this past week, and now, getting ready for Europe! Indeed, I am thoroughly appreciative of a fairly simple, but enjoyable life. How lucky, to be so independent, with, hopefully, many more years of the same to come! Time to rise and shine, albeit a bit earlier than usual, and have another great day.

But as I made the short walk from the bed to the bathroom, there was a tight, cramping sensation in my thighs, and my legs felt rubbery and weak. I walked as quickly as I could manage into the bathroom. Unable to control my balance, I finally flopped down on the toilet, making a banging noise on the landing. What could I have done the day before that would cause this? I had canceled tennis this day to get the last minute errands done for my trip, and had played three uneventful sets the day before, so no, not that. The little twinge in my back, when I lifted the garage door yesterday morning, and back discomfort during the day, was so insignificant, it had barely slowed me down. Anything else? Perhaps I had slept in an awkward position?

Get up, got to get going. Get up. Get up now.

I rubbed my thighs to the knees, but could not get rid of the tightness that felt like a rubber band stretched to the breaking point. Holding on to the window ledge and a small bath stand, I could barely pull myself up–much less walk–back to the end of the bed, without grasping on to everything stationary along the way. What could be happening?

Grab the phone; you aren't making it any further! Don't fall, hurry!

Then, as if a switch had been flipped, ripples of electric current felt as if they were radiating from my hips down, and I succumbed to the falling sensation. Holding the footboard of the bed, and the small bench that sat behind it, I came to rest gently on the rug at the foot of the bed. Staring at my legs, I could feel them attached to my body, but could not move them. They lay awkwardly on the floor in front of me, and seemed to suddenly be detached from my body, though I could feel them in place.

Move! Bend, knees, get these legs up!

Nothing. I tugged at my feet, massaging my thighs and calves. Nothing but burning numbness and tingling, as if my legs and behind were asleep and on fire. Why won't they work? This is so bizarre, and I do not have time for this craziness. I have things to do!

Stop, think. What could have caused my legs to quit working? Why do they feel this way? What did I do to cause this?

No trouble breathing, no chest pains, no nausea or dizziness, no headache, no vision issues, nothing that appeared like a stroke. Touching both arms, there were no strange or abnormal sensations there, no pain. I could not help but smile, as I said, "testing, one two" aloud, in an attempt to assess speech difficulty, of which there was none. I tried to crawl, but pulling dead weight is much harder than one would think. For a brief moment, I sat on the floor, stroking my legs and my sweet Annie, and stared mindlessly out the window. Maybe just sitting for a moment would help, right? But even then, I could not will my legs to move. How curious, as I felt fine in every other possible way. This could not be anything serious enough to slow me down for too long. Not me. Though my youngest daughter Gracyn, home from college for the summer, was in her room, I was sure no self-respecting student would be up at this hour, though I foolishly tried her cell phone, retrieving only voicemail. Of course, both my door and hers were closed. Grabbing a shoe from the nearby closet, and finally, my workout kettle bell, I threw the shoe at the door, followed by the rolling kettle bell that banged shamelessly against the door.

"Mom!" Gracyn rubbed her eyes and tousled her hair, as she stared down at me, crumpled on the floor like a ragdoll. "It's 5:30 on a Saturday! Really? Exercise at this hour?"

"I can't walk. I don't know what happened." Somehow, this was all I could manage.

"You can't walk? What do you mean?" Gracyn stared sternly at me, the disbelief, evident on her face, melted into fearful concern, as I relayed what had happened.

Poor Annie, who had cuddled affectionately beside me, did not fully understand all that was unfolding. Looking back, neither did I. At the time, maybe that was for the best.

The next several hours seemed to be a rush of people. Gracyn kept her wits about her, as if she were a medical professional, realizing the gravity of the situation, and calmly calling for help, though I could tell she was holding back some emotion. The first responders and ambulance crew never appeared ruffled or stressed about getting me down a flight of stairs. Strange, I gazed out the window of the ambulance, and remembered thinking that the rest of the city was going about the business of a regular Saturday, and that doctors would have me up and about in no time. I did not have time for this, and was just fine, otherwise, so this would all pass and things would be ok, I surmised. But that simply was not to be. Emergency room personnel assessed, with quiet calm, asking probing questions about prior illness, vaccines, unusual travel, injuries, spider bites, and the like. My oldest daughter, McKenna, drove as soon as she could from Ft. Mill, South Carolina, to the hospital, and remained focused and helpful. A host of concerned friends came as soon as I was placed in a room. And finally, later in the evening, the neurologist whose demeanor was calm, but whose words were as insidious as the pinpricks used to determine the level of damage throughout my body, delivered the devastating news that had lurked in the shadows all day, but was now a reality.

"Little lady, you won't be going to Europe, I'm afraid. Any trouble breathing? Is the paralysis just from the waist down? We are going to catheterize you, because you currently cannot control your bladder, nor bowels. Can you feel your arms? You might have Guillian-Barre syndrome, so if you notice any trouble breathing, or any ascending paralysis to the upper extremities, let us know immediately. We might need to put you on a ventilator. If recovery is even possible, it will be a long one. Not months, but years. At least two, perhaps more. You will need rehab to learn to manage a wheelchair, and so forth, in the mean time."

He patted my hand, and though he smiled, he now, at least to me, took on an almost hideous resemblance to Pennywise, the clown in Stephen King's "It", that bearer of nightmarish horror. He murmured something about the hospital taking good care of me. Then, he left as quickly as he had arrived, taking all happiness with him.

What the hell? A ventilator? Complete paralysis, at worst? Catheterization? A wheelchair, at best? Years to recover, if recovery was even possible?

The fear became grotesque and overwhelming, and I felt the tears rise, but fought them back. The words, however, ricocheted for a moment, deep inside my soul, throughout my body, then tumbled out with a vengeance.

"If that happens, I won't put my family through it. I'll get a damn gun first."

As soon as I had uttered the words, I imme-diately wished I had not. Not because I did not mean them in that moment, or cared who heard them – I did – but because I now had to give voice to the realization of what all of this meant. Something was wrong. Horribly, frighteningly, maybe permanently wrong. In a brief moment in time—for no apparent reason and without warning— life, as I knew it, had just metamorphosed from idyllic to insane. I closed my eyes and felt a nau-seating fear overtake me. The hot tears finally seeped out; slowly at first, then incessantly, like a waterfall, as I relinquished control to the insid-ious unknown.

What is happening to me? I am trapped in this hell, this broken body that, only days ago, was healthy—playing tennis, biking at the beach, walking in the mountains. What am I going to do if I can't be physically active? What will this do to my girls? What if I can never walk down a beach, travel the way I had planned, drive my sports car, or dance again? How could this be happening? My happy, fun life, as I knew it, was over. God, help me! Don't leave me! Please don't leave me.

Indeed, I felt like a child, in the worst kind of way, afraid of being left by a parent.

I was terrified about what could be happening to me, and the kind of life I might have to embrace. I had no choice but to hold on, with whatever strength and dignity I had left, to the promise that God Almighty would indeed help me out of this horror, somehow, in some kind of way. But make no mistake about it; I was frightened beyond comprehension, and perspective was now from an intensely dark and ominous place. There was no good to be found in this awful moment, and thoughts of finding a way to end my life had never been more real.

Finding Joy in the Hospital

Proverbs 17:22 A cheerful heart is good medicine, but a crushed spirit dries up the bones.

By the time that evening was closing in on my first day in the hospital, I had resigned myself to the fact that I was facing a devastating condition, whatever it was, and that I was in the fight of my life, and needed healing in a very big way. Definitely physical healing, but also spiritual healing, as I was reeling from the sucker-punch I had been dealt, and glad that I was not left alone, or given too much time to think. I could not move my legs at all, was completely incontinent, and my glutes and legs felt as if they were asleep

– only much more so – all the time, with no relief. I was told that this extreme numbness and tingling sensation was referred to as "paresthesia" and was indicative of nerve damage, but also a measure of some kind of sensation still intact, so not altogether a bad or good thing. I just knew it was incredibly uncomfortable. Gabapentin would be the medication of choice for such, and I did not relish the idea of taking it, but it was either take the medicine or feel like I was being stabbed; a burning, stinging ever-present sensation that was merely made less uncomfortable by succumbing to medication.

Thankfully, though, at least a semblance of my sense of humor had begun to return, as I fought to bring any kind of normalcy back into my life. I would indeed be in need of it, as by the end of the second day, I had been asked to endure three MRI's, to rule out everything from spinal compression, to multiple sclerosis, and even cancer. Ben and Dave, the wonderful technicians at Baptist Hospital, kept me apprised of any World Cup Soccer or Wimbledon happenings that I might have missed while having these procedures done, which certainly made the pro-cedures more bearable. Because of my claustro-phobia, medication was given each time to help me relax as much as possible, before entering what I not-so-affectionately called "the Pringles can" or the MRI machine. Having that much med-ication in one day ultimately resulted in a very low heart rate, and–while I kept telling them it was unnecessary – also a one-day move to the car-diac floor to be sure my heart rate was stabilized. The following day, I was returned to my original floor, and a beautiful, nicely appointed room, with a view of the city, and full of flowers, plants, and cards from a host of friends and well-wishers. It was so worth the move!

Finally, a doctor came in my room to explain what would be my first diagnosis. MRIs revealed unexplained inflammation present at the T-10 level in my spine, which is in the lower thoracic region. As a result of the location of the trauma, the paralysis was confined to everything across and below the injury level; thus, my hips, legs, buttocks, and genital areas were all impacted. Thankfully, the upper region of my body, especially respiratory function, as well as arm and core strength, remained intact. Because I could still feel touch, feel my legs, and sense a measure of hot and cold temperatures, my injury was deemed to be incomplete, as opposed to a complete injury, in which no sensation or movement is present. I was told I had transverse myelitis, or inflammation that transcends the area across the entire spinal cord at the designated level of injury. All of this information was overwhelming, at best; but worse, there was no viable explanation for what could have caused the inflammation. There were possible culprits noted in other cases of this rare occurrence, such as tick bites, recent vaccinations, or other injury. Since I had not experienced any of these in a way that concerned hospital physicians, my diagnosis was listed as idiopathic transverse myelitis, which indicated an unknown cause. I was both fascinated and terrified that one could be walking one moment and paralyzed within minutes, and for no apparent reason. The reality has served as a stark reminder that, in this life, we are not guaranteed strife-free living, and that tragedy, in all of its many forms, can and does happen.

For some reason, all of this conjured up a memory of a moment in my childhood – I could not have been more than six years old, or so – when I began to grapple with this very notion. As I recall, I had overheard my mother use the phrase, "when I kick the bucket", in a playful reference to her no longer being alive. While it was said in jest, of course, my overactive and vivid imagination kicked into high gear, and I spent an extremely inordinate amount of time pondering the idea that she could actually die. That night, my parents hosted a bridge party, complete with card tables set up all across our den. Way past my bedtime, I stood in my pajamas and peeked through the doorway, observing all the food, beverages, and merriment. I remember never wanting that sense of security to disappear from my young life, and I was suddenly overcome with the fear that my mom could actually die. When the terror was more than I could bear, I tore into the den, in tears, and declared, in front of all of the guests, that I did not want her to "kick the bucket".

Needless to say, I neither understood, nor cared, about the smiles, the murmured "aw, isn't that sweet", nor the ensuing jests that followed. All I knew was that it was possible to lose something very important to me, and that I would never be alright again, if that happened.

To this day, I do not remember her exact words, but I do remember that she took me into another room, held me on her lap, and assured me, in some way, that she had no plans to kick the proverbial bucket any time soon, and that we should not worry about things that could happen in our lives, over which we had no control. If we did so, we would spend most of our lives worrying. Words to live by, indeed, as I reflect on this childhood memory, in wake of where I am in this moment. Now, I cannot help but be thankful that I did not spend all of my prior years worrying about what could happen, but made good memories that will sustain me through whatever I must endure. More importantly, I know that always – always – I must choose joy, even in the midst of great pain, because that is part of who God intends for me to be. I used to think that joy was

*simply an emotion to be felt when I am happy –
and it is that. But, it is so much more. Claiming
joy is not always easy, nor fun, as paradoxical as
that may sound. Sometimes, it is an act of faith
in the darkness, rather than a reaction to the exu-
berance of life. Sometimes, it is doing all one can,
and then thanking God and waiting on Him to do
the rest. It is learning to smile through the tears,
when the reality of life feels insurmountable. And
it is this knowledge that I hope will sustain me to
the end of my days.*

*While in the hospital, encouragement – and
joy–came in many forms, and seemingly at times
when I needed them most. One of the most memorable of those times was when I met Wendy. She
walked into my room, completely unannounced,
and stood at the foot of my bed, smiling. A little
younger than I, she was blonde, petite, and
walked with an only slightly detectable hitch in
her gait.*

*"Hi, I'm Wendy," she said, "and I am a nurse
here in this hospital. I heard about you from your
nurse tech, Debra, and I had to come see you. A
few years ago, I received a flu vaccine, and within*

days, could not walk. It is rare, but I, too, was diagnosed with transverse myelitis, given lots of steroids at first. I could not walk for several weeks, and could not work for quite some time. I'm still recovering. Two years now. But I'm back at work. And I know a guy across town that also faced a similar outcome. He said I could give you his name and number. We are both walking now. Perhaps with a limp, or with a cane, or sometimes a walker, but we are both on our feet. Both of us went through a great deal of physical therapy and extremely hard work, with lots of tears and fears. I just wanted to say that you should never give up, and that I know how hard this is and will be for you. But, I mostly wanted you to see what may be possible."

To say that I was amazed by her presence at a time when I most needed encouragement would be a tremendous understatement. I remember feeling humbled and thankful, and crying just at the thought of perhaps being able to walk again. Could it be that I might overcome this adversity and one day walk on a beach again, or feel my feet pushing the pedals on my little red car? Maybe even serve a tennis ball again, or feel my body dance? At least, there was hope. We talked about what happened to her, the stages of her recovery. It was indeed helpful to talk with someone who had experienced a measure of the craziness that had invaded my life. At least I had the strength to face another day.

Another piece of joy came in the form of quite a few instances of much-needed humor. My room was on the eighth floor of the hospital, which was actually divided into two distinct sections. Years ago, the eighth floor in this hospital was a locked psychiatric ward. So, at first, I was a bit flustered when a patient – a man appearing to be a few years older than I–gray, disheveled looking– appeared at my door and stood extremely still, simply staring at me. A nurse quickly got him under wraps, and explained that this floor was now often a bit of an overflow from other floors, and that he sometimes wandered a bit, but was harmless. I guessed him to be perhaps a veteran, with some signs of PTSD, or maybe some traumatic brain injury. I wished, only for a second, to trade him my legs for his mind, whatever he might be thinking. One evening, he visited me again. Same as before, merely standing in my room, staring through me, at something I could not see. It was quite frightening, at first. I decided to take matters into my own control, as quickly as possible.

"Hey," I said to him as softly as I could. "You know, there are people out there looking for you. It's not safe in here or out in the hall. They have nets, you know. It would be a lot safer for you in your very own room. I'm concerned for you, ok?"

With that, he stared at me for a minute longer, never uttered a word, turned around, and walked out. I never saw him again. A nurse later told me that he was no longer walking around; that he seemed to choose to remain in his room unless escorted out. She wondered aloud what made him choose to do so. I just smiled and said I was glad he had settled down.

Another such incident occurred in the middle of the night. I had been sleeping soundly, thanks to the effects of medication – ah, better living through chemistry, right?–when two women in scrubs, one a good bit taller than the other, quietly *entered my room and asked if I were asleep. Of course, if I had been, I was not any longer. But barely awake, I heard one of them say that they were from the maternity team.*

"The maternity team?" I asked incredulously.

I tried to sit up, could not help but smile – at least these gals did not want any blood or vitals taken. Did they not have my birth date written anywhere to assure them that someone on the verge of sixty years old certainly should be past those days? I mean, just keep on walking past this door, please, and let me get some of that illusive sleep! But they were not leaving.

"Ladies, I am hell and gone from being anywhere near needing a maternity team."

There, that ought to do it.

With that, they began laughing uncontrollably, holding on to one another for support. One finally managed to breathe enough to tell me that they were not from the maternity team, but, rather from the "Turn Team", as they were so designated, since it was their job to visit paralyzed patients to see if they needed assistance turning from one position to another. Cue up my turn to laugh, which I desperately needed to do. At least, I had made some new friends and could go to sleep thinking about my own precious girls, when I had actually spent time in the maternity ward of this very hospital. Perhaps happiness will not be so far away. At least not now.

After this night, I was able to focus more on each person that came in and out of my room, from nurses and technicians, to friends, my priest, our choir director, chaplains, florist delivery folks, and the like. All welcomed, and all came with words of encouragement. None were afraid to ask what exactly had happened, how I was feeling in that moment. And I was very glad that they did, as it allowed me the opportunity to vent some, to tell my story in my own way, much as a child makes sense of his or her world through play and repetition of the storyline. The retelling of it all was quite therapeutic, and on occasion, someone pointed me in the direction of pertinent research, which gave me an added sense of purpose, and a challenge to tackle, in discovering anything that might help me and my family make sense of all that had transpired, as well as what was to come. Of course, it was suggested that I consider writing a book about this most rare and frightening experience. I knew it was something that I should do, for no other reason than to help someone else in a similar circumstance. But all I could do in the early days would be to take brief descriptive notes for use later. Getting better was the most important goal, and I was certainly overwhelmed with future prospects.

Divine Debra and The
Fourth of July

Job 2:11 "When Job's three friends…heard about the troubles that had come upon him, they set out from their homes and met together by agreement to go and sympathize with him and comfort him."

B y the time July 4, 2014, rolled around, I had been in the Baptist Hospital one week – with no shower or shampoo – and was beginning to feel the effects of being just plain dirty, having to be catheterized, and bedridden for the entire time, moved briefly to another room and now getting ready to be moved yet again. Not to mention the fact that I was also frustrated that my much anticipated trip to Germany, Austria, and Switzerland simply was not going to happen. I had taken such great care to contact the church secretary in St. Margrethen, Switzerland, to arrange a tour of the tiny church, where my first known ancestor on my mother's side was baptized in 1706. We had maintained such amiable correspondence, that she had graciously offered to pick us up at the rail station when we arrived from Germany, though we had never met. I had even purchased a book of South Carolina photos and history for her. Trying to arrange the refund of my tickets and passes, all while battling paralysis, was becoming grueling, as well. While I had managed to maintain a fairly positive demeanor, the frustration was beginning to mount, and I had become weepy in the early hours of that particular morning.

Enter, amazing nurse technician Debra. I had taken a liking to her as soon as I met her on my very first day in the hospital. Sturdy in stature, with long, wavy black hair, and ebony skin that appeared to be smooth as glass, she was a one-woman team, taking care of every possible patient need, sometimes even before a request was made. It was almost as if she had a stage persona – feisty, humorous, with an effervescence of vernacular and grit. Yet, in a blink, she could transform into a no-nonsense, quiet lady of faith, strength, and articulate manners. A good soul, to be sure. As soon as she came in my room on this day, she stood still, put both hands on her hips, and stared at me.

"What's wrong, baby? I can tell something ain't right! You know we're taking you to a new room, back with us?" Debra squinted both eyes in that daring kind of way that let me know she wanted a straight up answer.

"I don't know. I guess I'm just tired of being paralyzed already. Hell, I can't even go to the bathroom on my own. I can barely sit on the edge of the bed without losing my balance. Because of the catheter, I had a urinary tract infection I didn't even know I had. And I haven't had a shower. Yeah, I guess that and I'm just scared." By the end of that sentence, I was aware that my voice had tapered down to a whisper. With that, honest tears crept out and I let her see the fear that I

kept trying to push away. Debra wasted no time in closing the door to my room with such authority that I doubted anyone would cross her. Walking back to my bed, she took both of my hands in hers.

"Now look here. Look at me. You been positive all this here time. You gonna be ok. I can take care of getting you cleaned up, but we gotta take care of something bigger, first. Let's pray."

I knew she was not inviting me to join her, but rather commanding me to seek something greater than my own strength, which seemed about null and void at this point. I closed my eyes and listened intently to her soothing and reassuring voice, and felt my spirit beg for some kind of respite from this living nightmare. Debra was undaunted by my moment of frailty.

"Lord God, our heavenly Father, you fill our needs even before we ask it of you. You give strength where there is weakness You quiet the stormy waters in the midst of all our fears. You are the Great Physician who heals our spirits and our bodies of all infirmity. Look down on your servant, Pat, with kindness. In your own time and in your own way, teach her to wait. And when the time is *right, in accordance with your will, restore her to the fullness of your heavenly grace. We ask this in the blessed name of Jesus Christ, Your Most Precious Son. Amen."*

With that, Debra opened her eyes, but continued to hold my hands.

"Baby, you just gotta learn to wait and be patient. This is gonna take awhile. God loves you. Trust Him. You know Debra ain't gonna tell you no lies." She didn't wait for me to respond.

"Now," she looked around the room, "I need a bedpan to wash you up good, after a bite of breakfast. I hear you got a bunch of company coming up in here later to help you celebrate July 4. Tomorrow, the morning folks can get you a real shower. You with me now?" I smiled through tears at her.

"Yes, m'am, I am. Lead the way."

Debra left temporarily while breakfast was delivered, but came back with all of the accoutrements for a bedside wash. With speed and finesse, she soaked me, the bed, and likely much of the floor, with warm, soapy water. Using a cloth, she gently wiped my hair, just enough to call it damp, and applied a mere drop of shampoo, and quickly massaged my head. I couldn't help but laugh, in the midst of more tears.

"Girl, now what?" Debra smiled knowingly, but had her hands on her hips again, and her eyebrows raised in feigned frustration. "Lawd have mercy!"

"Debra, it's just so good to feel clean! I was pretty ripe! And everyone else kept telling me I had to wait. I can't thank you enough."

"Who, everyone else?" Debra demanded in a semi-angry kind of way. "Never mind, don't even tell me. Debra's got you now, and that's all that matters." With that, she grabbed up all of the wet towels, mopped up the floor, and rushed back in with dry bed sheets.

"How are we going to do this?" I asked, wondering if I needed to be moved from the bed. "Do you need someone to help you move me?"

Debra raised an eyebrow at me. "Now, Pat. You know I got this. If I need anybody else, I'll call 'em." With that, she hustled me from one side of the bed to the other, pulling on sheets with the precision of a drill sergeant, until I had a freshly made bed, with me comfortably in it.

"Debra, I don't even know what to say," I gushed, "You're just the best."

"Well," Debra said with quiet confidence, "Ain't nobody around here work like I do. You got Debra, you got the best. So, your room is ready and you got people up there, so let's get on it."

She maneuvered the bed through a corridor or two, to an elevator, and eventually back to my original floor. Much to my surprise, the beautifully appointed and spacious room, with the softest green walls and a large window facing down-town Columbia and Finlay Park, had many floral arrangements and balloons that had been deliv-ered before I got there. It was already decked out for the Fourth of July holiday, with a large banner, sparkler-inspired decorations, and a picnic buffet of barbecue, ribs, slaw, beans, and apple pie. Music was gently humming from an ipod-type player, and there were fixings for Bloody Marys and a cooler with beer.

As I looked around the room, I saw my brother, Hank and wife Monica, and a roomful of mostly tennis friends, drinks in hand, ready to party. Tears came again, and I remember feeling incredibly fortunate to have people take time out of their celebrations to come down to the hospital to spend a few minutes with me. It was all pretty overwhelming, as I gladly accepted a Bloody Mary, with a beer chaser on the side. How fun to feel normal again, for a few minutes! As I was being served food, I heard Debra mumble something to my brother – who is the master of practical jokes and good humor – about not wearing me out; that I was a bit emotional, with all I had going on. She must have said something that fired him up, as he had some kind of funny exchange with her that I could not hear. I did, however, hear her tell him to "bring it" at some point and bow up with one hand on her hip, and one finger waving and pointing at him, Aretha Franklin-style, as her head bobbed and weaved in true diva fashion. It was fairly obvious to all that Hank had met his match in Divine Debra. The thought of the two of them engaged in verbal sparring made me smile.

After all had left, and evening was well underway, I saw fireworks in the distance, through the window. Rolling on my side, and working hard to pull my legs in place, I took a moment to take it all in. I was supposed to be in Germany right about now. Time to let that go, I guess. The last thing I remember, before asking God again to stay with me, is that perhaps one can't see such beauty as fireworks, until there is complete darkness. At least tonight, I would sleep better; and the challenges of tomorrow would be there, just the same.

The next morning, Debra was there, as promised, and spent a few minutes telling me all about her family cookout. It sounded as though she was the matriarch of them all – no surprise there.

"So, how did that shower go?" she beamed, assuming I had been given one.

"The two nurses that came in here earlier said they could not do it; that they just did not have enough personnel today. But it's ok, Debra, you got me through yesterday." I said sincerely enough. However Debra was unfazed.

"What? No, that ain't ok at all, damn it. I got you through yesterday, but you are due a shower – a real one – and you are gonna have it!"

She raised her chin defiantly, as if to dare the naysayers to contradict her. Marching quickly out of my room, I listened for her to start taking names and kicking some proverbial behind. The thought brought a smile to my face, though I was somewhat worried about Debra trying to take on more than she could manage, just to try to prove a point. Within minutes, she was back in my room with a surplus of white towels, forcefully closing the door once again. She lowered my bed and disengaged every possible attachment to my body. Then, she gently assisted me in sitting on the edge of the bed, with my legs dangling over the side, useless. I felt so helpless, not even being able to balance well to sit on the edge of the bed. How strange, the effects of paralysis.

"Now," she directed, "Here's how we gonna do this. I'm gonna hold you under your arms and around your waist, and you are gonna put your arms around my neck. Together, we gonna get you into this wheelchair and into the shower, ok?"

I nodded obediently, and did exactly as Debra asked. As promised, by herself, she got me into a wheelchair designed for a shower. Within minutes, she had me in the open shower, the water adjusted just right, and my head full of shampoo. Handing me the spray attachment, she gently said that I could take as long as I wanted, and that she would sit in a plastic chair with her back to me, so that I would not be alone. To say that the experience was life-changing may be a bit of an exaggeration – but not much. I cried silent, heartfelt tears, realizing just how good the warmth of the water felt, completely drenching my entire body with a measure of comfort. More importantly, I knew then, for a brief moment, an inkling of how much my life was getting ready to change. But for now, all I needed to know was that Debra had done the impossible, and in so doing, had shown me a kindness far beyond her calling. I made sure she had plenty of time to rest while I had a nice long shower. A win for both of us.

When Debra told me she had days off coming up, I knew I would likely not see her again before I was moved to Health South for rehabilitation. I also knew that she had done more for me than any doctor thus far. I knew that she had enjoyed my company, as much as I had needed hers. I wrote to hospital management about how much she had helped me, and gone far beyond her job description in making me feel safe and comfortable. I felt sad the day I left the hospital, on July 7, 2014, and knew that I would never forget her – and hoped that maybe, one day, I could literally walk back into her life to tell her again how much she had helped me make it through some dark and difficult days.

What would I have done without the divine care of all who were sent my way?

Inpatient Rehabilitation
– Three Weeks at Health South Rehab Facility

James 1:12 Blessed is the one who perseveres under trial, because, having stood the test, that person will receive the crown of life that the Lord has promised to those who love Him."

July 7, 2014, was bittersweet, and incredibly hot. It was the first time I had been outside in nine days. I was finally leaving Baptist Hospital, albeit still paralyzed, but in the hopes of making progress with some intensive inpatient physical therapy. I was driven across town by ambulance, still catheterized, and admitted to yet another hospital-type room, alongside a much older, heavy-set, jovial woman named Dolly. Now Dolly had suffered a stroke, and was near the end of her recovery period here at Health South. Though she was a charming and sweet woman, she was, as my grandfather would have noted, "a bit of a talker", chatting incessantly about her health issues, her family, and her upcoming trip back home. I was, of course, happy for her, but happier still to be able to claim the entire room as private, as nurses had indicated that, due to the nature of my paralysis, they had arranged for the room to be just for me. I must say, I would not miss Dolly's TV that remained on into the wee hours – and set loudly on the cartoon network!

My first day at Health South was largely spent getting settled into my new room and learning what the upcoming routine would be. Physical therapy would be intensive, paired with occupational therapy, and would last several hours a day, everyday, with the exception of one weekend day. All of my flowers and cards that were still alive were transferred to my new room and helped to create a nice sense of transition and homey comfort. I had also continued my habit of daily morning devotionals and evening prayers, and would do so here in this place. They helped me to remain focused on God, rather than on myself, and to draw strength needed for all the recovery work. A doctor came by, in the early evening, to review my diagnosis, and explain that my stay here would be approximately three weeks to a month in duration. At the time, I thought nine days in a hospital would do me in, but the thought of up to a month, even in a rehab hospital, such as this one, was overwhelming, at best. I was told that I could eat in my room, or enjoy a meal brought in by a friend, at any time. I certainly did take advantage of that, many times over, as friends, former colleagues, my daughters and other family members, and members of my church would all bring meals to share, either outside on a picnic deck area, or inside a common area room that provided a nice distraction from the confines and trappings of a hospital room. Cards, letters, flowers, and visits continued two-fold here, and I felt humbly blessed to have such loving people in my life.

The first full morning of physical therapy, the catheter was finally removed, for which I was eternally grateful, but perhaps with a rather big caveat. Having formerly been a Danskin-type of underwear gal – that's very thin, soft, and comfortable material, for those that don't know – I was utterly horrified to learn that I would now have to wear a hospital version of Depends, or something similar. Mind you, not the smaller, modest "pad" version, but rather the full coverage, could-hold-a-leak-in-the-Hoover Dam type of underwear. To say that I was frustrated and hugely uncomfortable was a gargantuan understatement. This part was every bit an obstacle to handle as much as the paralysis. Not to mention the actual rolling from side-to-side in my bed just to pull those horrible things on, in addition to the yoga-type pants for physical therapy. Getting dressed was proving to be a tiring adventure in its own right. I silently fumed, while being helped into a wheelchair and rolled down to the sprawling physical therapy area. I hated every minute of being in what amounted to an adult diaper, as far as I was concerned. Was it not enough that I could not stand or walk? Now,

I had to suffer the indignity of feeling years older than I was. I was falling deeper into the abyss of self-pity – that most dangerous of emotions – when we rounded the corner to the elevator that would take us downstairs to therapy. Above one of the doors was a sign that read:

"You might not remember the first time you learned to walk; but, you will never forget the second."

It quite literally took my breath away for a brief moment, and it seemed that the tears welling up in my eyes also simply refused to fall. I stared at it, suspended in that moment, wondering how long, if ever, would that time be for me. With certainty, I also knew that recovering the precious gift of being able to stand and walk would be worth every difficult moment it took to achieve that lofty goal. I think it was then that I solidified my dedication to whatever it took to get better, and shook off doubt and worry, at least for now. As we entered the inpatient therapy area, I silently prayed for strength and guidance to face this day.

I had arrived early, so I sat parked in my chair and observed Rich, who would be my physical *therapist. I guessed him to be in his thirties; light reddish brown hair, in an updated and nice bowl-type cut, physically fit, with a pleasant demeanor. He moved with a quiet calm, appearing to impart the same to those with whom he worked. When it was my turn, Rich showed me the nuances of moving and turning the wheelchair. We went on what I was certain to be the general "guided tour" of the great room, with me executing all of the proper ways to navigate the chair before Rich suggested we venture outside to a slight upward grade on a sidewalk. While learning to maneuver the ups and downs of sidewalks, and so forth, Rich asked for details about what had happened to me. Again, I got to share, in painstaking detail, the whole sordid tale. When I was done, he regarded me with a rather quizzical expression, and said that he had never heard of anything quite like that before. It figures. Only me.*

I did my best to smile and boldly state that my goal was to walk again, no matter how long it might take. Rich reminded me that nerve damage such as mine would take quite a long time to heal, if healing was even possible. I assured him I knew that, but my plan was not changing. With that, we went back inside and I was more than grateful to engage in weightlifting and the use of an arm aerobic machine. I felt exhilarated and new again. I would work this room into a frenzy. Beast mode all the way. Do more than the minimum required. Physical therapy, I could and would embrace wholeheartedly.

Occupational therapy, however, proved to be somewhat different. I surmised that Jessica, my therapist, was perhaps late twenties to thirties, pretty, with black hair, fair, creamy skin, and deep set blue eyes, with a no-nonsense approach to getting it done. The first order of the day was learning to transfer from my wheelchair to the raised therapy mat, or bed. This was not as easy or as much fun as working out in the gym, and it served as a reminder of my handicapping condition. Nevertheless, I knew that I would be walking – perhaps this term is a bit of an overstatement for now, but you get the idea – a very fine line between learning to accommodate my new life in a wheelchair, while working incessantly to get out of it for good, so I gave the effort all I could muster, and then some. Pushing against my hands, doing the best I could to lift my backside up from the chair and onto the mat – all without the assistance of my legs or feet, which were deadweights at this point – proved to be a challenge, largely due to issues of balance. I now better understood why it was so critical to develop a strong upper body. Rich would also practice this with me. He also gently reminded that being confined to a wheelchair meant that I was not burning calories as efficiently, and that, unless I wanted to gain weight – which I most assuredly did not, as I had needed to lose some weight before this happened – I needed to cut my intake of food greatly, and be sure that there were no wasted calories on junk food.

A few days later, Dr. Petit, who I discovered was not only a physician, but also an Episcopal priest, spent a good amount of time explaining that there were several things I could do to improve my general health and give my body a better chance to heal, since the diagnosis of transverse myelitis involved inflammation of some kind. I apparently had significant Vitamin D and C deficiencies, as many people do, so I was given mega-doses of those essentials. I was also strongly encouraged to give up diet cokes and any kind of artificial sweeteners. Basically, Dr. Petit explained that, when one eats artificial sweeteners, the body is not being metabolically satisfied, so the cravings for sugar increases greatly; thus, it is common for one to then load up on calorie-rich foods, which totally defeats the purpose of the artificial sweeteners and actually ends up doing more harm than good. He actually bet me that, if I would give up artificial sweeteners, and use just honey in moderation, or organic stevia, a natural sweetener, while I remained in inpatient rehab, I would lose not only the craving for diet coke, but that I would lose weight, as well, by the time I went home. He won that bet, I am happy to report, and I have not had a diet coke since then. And an even better aside – I am not nearly as hungry, and feel much better! Perhaps more importantly, Dr. Petit never made me feel like there was no hope for the possibility of being able to walk again. Though realistic in his approach, recognizing that no one could guarantee what the future would hold, he was firm and resolute in his belief that God would carry me.

"He's brought you this far, so you don't think He's going to drop you now, do you?" he smiled warmly, while noting just a twinge of movement in one of my knees.

Such a simple question. But it challenged my faith in a profound way. Did I really believe God would and has always sustained me, whether or not I ever walked again? Was it ok to keep asking God for the precious gift of returning my ability to walk? Could I commit to trusting God, through this long and strenuous journey, knowing that extremely tough times were not going to be absent from my life? I knew I had to decide. I was slowly learning that real faith is no part-time venture for sissies.

One of the biggest challenges I had was not losing hope. On one of the first days in rehab, a social worker came to my room to make the obligatory mental health visit. Interestingly, he was in a wheelchair, as well, and stated that his condition was permanent, but that he had learned to manage quite well, as I would. He handed me a *book about learning to live in a wheelchair, and talked incessantly about adapting to my new life, the detailed process of self-catheterization for females, and jumping back into the dating game. Immediately, I felt a bristling sense of panic begin to rise in my throat, and fought back the tears that were trying to erupt, along with a desperate and fatal fear.*

"You need to shut the hell up!" I silently screamed at him, while trying to formulate a kinder response.

"Look, I know that you mean well, and that you want me to be realistic about my condition. But I feel like you want me to let go of any hope that I will ever get better, and I can't do that, right now. As for self-catheterization, I'm not going to do it. I'm managing without it. And dating is certainly not on my agenda right now, and it doesn't need to be."

He looked at me with concern, and something that resembled pity, which I most definitely did not want. As a licensed professional counselor myself, I recognized the attempt to help me focus on the here and now. But I also knew the importance of meeting someone where he or she was, in their personal journey, to make sense of tragedy and formulate choices. I never felt that this caregiver truly was able to understand the nature of my rare injury–for lack of a better term of reference to call this bizarre thing that had happened to me – nor did he understand where I was, emotionally. While he could be right, I was not ready to accept that my condition was permanent. What a lesson was reinforced that day! I promised myself, as a mental health professional, to always be sure clients acknowledged my understanding of not only their feelings, but also all that their journey entailed. In the end, the social worker agreed that I would tell him when I wanted to talk. Though he truly wanted to help, of that, I am certain, I never contacted him again. And I never read the how-to-be-handicapped book that was placed on the counter in my room. When I eventually left the facility for good, I left the book, along with the initial self-catheterization kit that was provided, lying on my bed. But hope, I would take with me.

Dr. Petit checked on his patients constantly, both in physical therapy and in room visits. One day during a room visit, he surprised me by saying that he was not sure transverse myelitis was my correct diagnosis. He recommended a procedure, called plasmapheresis, that might help make a difference, if transverse myelitis was the right diagnosis. At best, the procedure would help me get better. At worse, even if the procedure did not produce positive results, it might help rule out the diagnosis I had. The Red Cross would bring the necessary equipment to my room and per-form the procedures: five, in all, and done every other day. Very similar to a dialysis-like proce-dure, blood would be removed from my body via an IV in one arm, the plasma separated out and antibodies that may be attacking the immune system removed, and then other plasma, or a plasma substitute, along with blood, is returned to the body via an IV in another arm. Each proce-dure should last about an hour. A rather lengthy and involved endeavor, but a risk I was willing to take. I agreed immediately, as there was nothing to lose, and everything to gain. It would take time, and a little bit of red tape, to get everything in place. I would wait and remain hopeful.

When day one finally arrived, the nurse from the Red Cross that would be doing the procedure greeted me warmly. As good fortune would have it, Carolyn and I discovered that we were once at Crayton Junior High School – now referred to as middle school – together, and we reminisced about friends and the brief years there. Carolyn was such a kind, gentle, and caring soul, that she was able to readily put me at ease for the duration of treatment. She worked skillfully, her hands moving quickly and deliberately among the buttons, IV lines, and containers, and I marveled at her quiet confidence in all that she did. The entire time she was present, talk was effortless and relaxed, even when the antiquated equipment would not cooperate. Unfortunately, malfunctions were prevalent, and she had to make frequent adjustments to IV lines – not pleasant, but we both managed – and reset equipment functions. Because of the frequency of the problems encountered, more time was required for the entire process. As a result, each of the five required days took two to three hours to complete, instead of the normal one hour. Even though I was lying quietly, and remained completely immobile, the end of each procedure left me exhausted.

On the fourth and next to the last procedure, I could tell that Carolyn was frustrated that the equipment was so finicky. She maneuvered, cajoled, and readjusted as best she could, to no avail. We both grew weary of the bells and pings that constantly alerted one to malfunctions, and prolonged an agonizing regrouping of sorts. As best practice dictates, she wisely decided to call in reinforcements. Within an hour, I was amazed to see a massive, sculpted, and good-looking young black man, in a fitted black t-shirt and khaki pants come striding into my room. He smiled, exuding an aura of confidence and coolness, as well, and introduced himself as Nate. Intuition told me I would like him immediately, despite the fact that the idea of a 'nurse' usually conjured up a female for me. Ah, the times, they are a-changing! Of course, I should have guessed that he had played college football, just by his physique alone. Finding out that he had graced the gridiron of Williams Brice Stadium as a cornerback for my beloved University of

South Carolina Gamecocks was an added treat. While Nate attempted to work his magic, we discussed football players, coaches, seasons, and some behind-the-scenes tidbits of team fun. All of these meanderings kept me grounded and focused on getting through this most difficult process. But what really endeared Nate to me was his unabashed willingness to speak his faith. Not in a proselytizing, in-your-face, hellfire and damnation religious fervor, but rather from a place of honest and believable normalcy. He spoke his truth simply, referencing his faith, his family, his own struggles, and his joy for this life in a way that revealed both humanity and conviction of character. He kept encouraging me to never give up the fight to get better, no matter how long I had to keep working toward that goal – and to always remember that God promises to work for the good when we persevere in faith. What a cool guy.

On the fifth and final day of plasmapheresis, Nate came again and remained for the entire three-hour procedure, though he was not required to do so. My, how those young female nurses monitored my room frequently, checking

*Nate out, and trying to maintain their profession-
alism. Observing them gave me at least moments
of levity. Both Nate and Carolyn worked tirelessly
to get everything running smoothly and to keep
me comfortable for the duration of the procedure.
Admittedly, the last day was difficult, as I was
physically worn out, both from the repeated procedures, and from the many times needles had
to be reinserted into my arms for better circula-
tion. I only watched once, as the blood flowed
continuously from one arm, through the machine,
back to my other arm, and decided my squea-
mish side was better off without entertainment.
Thankfully, all ended well, and Nate and Carolyn
offered heartfelt wishes for success. Carolyn and
I exchanged contact information and she gave
me a pair of turquoise earrings that she had made,
along with a matching beaded bracelet. I put them
all on and would wear them for the next few days.*

*After we said our goodbyes, I let a nurse help
me into my bathroom. I promptly got back into
bed and slept through dinner, not waking until
the following morning, when an aide came to
remind me that I had physical therapy. Of course,*

common sense should have dictated that I rest on this day, but I insisted on engaging in full-blown stubborn mode and said I was up for it. As luck would have it, my regular therapist, Rich, was not there, and I had a handsome, young substitute therapist who knew nothing about the procedures I had just endured. Perfect.

Why, yes, of course I would like to lift weights today, and then get into the standing machine! In fact, I can lift weights while I am in the machine, too, just because I can!

And so I did. Being cranked into a standing position, supported by straps and braces, was the most exhilarating feeling. How I had cried, the first time I was hoisted up to an almost-standing position, after a month of not being able to do so! I could relate to Kate Winslet's character in the scene in Titanic, where she is standing on the bow of the ship and has the sensation of flying. I often referred to that machine as, "the Titanic". Today was no different. For several minutes, I grinded away at the eight pound weights, working my biceps, then triceps, and began working on deltoids, when colors began to fade to gray, and consciousness slipped slowly away. I reluctantly called for help – at least I am pretty sure I did.

Damn it. Yep, overdone it, didn't you? That wasn't very smart. But you had to keep pushing yourself. The words kept replaying in my head. Too late now.

"Pat? Can you hear me?" The cute physical therapist was touching my cheek, feeling my forehead, as a white-coated physician hovered overhead, stethoscope at the ready. I was lying on one of the raised therapy mats, with a crowd of staff gathered around.

"I fainted, didn't I?" I managed to whisper, while trying to smile.

The impromptu strategy worked temporarily, as all of the staff appeared relieved. The doctor, however, regained his more somber approach, and asked what had happened. He mentioned something about heart rate and blood pressure being low and that, perhaps hospital observation might be needed. At that point, I coughed up my foolishness and admitted that I had pushed myself too hard. He shook his head, and muttered something about that not being a behavior they saw in rehab too often. But at least he was smiling now, as he gave strict instructions to stay on the mat for the remainder of the hour and that my vitals needed to be monitored before I could get back in my wheelchair. He called me 'young miss' – which I thoroughly enjoyed – and insisted that I could not do any rehab for the next day. I mindlessly fidgeted with my new turquoise bracelet, on the return trip to my room, as I received a free push from an attending aide. When I had gotten settled back in bed, I picked up my devotional reading for the day. It was a reading from Isaiah 54:11.

"Afflicted city, lashed by storms and not comforted, I will rebuild you with stones of turquoise, your foundations with lapis lazuli."

I would rest well that night, after replenishing my body with nourishing food, and I would sleep with my new bracelet all night.

It Happens
(the hardest chapter to write)

Matthew 27:46 "My God, My God, why have you forsaken me?"

Luke 23:46 "Jesus called out with a loud voice, 'Father, into your hands I commit my spirit."

"*So, you were catheterized for nine days in the hospital, right? And you don't have much bladder and bowel control? You will need to learn how to do digital stimulation, or digi-stim, as we call it, which is manually making your-self poop.*"

Jessica, the young occupational therapist, stared at me, her face void of emotion, as if to keep me from dwelling on the indignity of such a prospect. She explained, in brief clinical terms, about using a medical glove with personal lubricant, to insert a finger into one's own anus. It was to be conducted gently by moving the finger in a circular motion to create peristalsis, or the contraction and relaxation of muscles to facilitate defecation.

"Just ask a nurse for some gel and gloves, and give it a try." Jessica smiled, her eyebrows manicured and brushed into submission, highlighted intense eyes that attempted to convince me this act was both normal and easy.

I smiled back, assuring her that I would be fine with the attempt, but it was a performance worthy of an Academy Award, as I was inwardly horrified by the idea. Self-catheterization, I did not have to do, but there was no choice, with digital stimulation. I tried to smile. The name of the procedure sounded very pornographic, to me. At least I could smile at that! After dinner, when all was still and quiet, I forced myself to procure the required gloves and gel, and managed to wheel myself into the bathroom and slide onto the toilet without falling. So far so good. A well-meaning nurse stopped by to check on me and closed the bathroom door. It was in that moment that I began to feel the uneasiness creeping from the pit of my stomach, up through my throat. A brief wave of nausea followed, and I forced it back with several long, deep breaths.

"I can do this," I said aloud, trying to smile at my own ineptness and reluctance to engage in this act. The glove and gel went on effortlessly enough. I held my right hand in front of my face, studying it for what seemed like several minutes, trying to envision myself carrying this act to completion. With my index finger, I began the insertion. Though I had limited sensation there, I could feel my finger become coated in warmth; a visceral thickness that seemed to ooze forever. Instinctively, I pulled my hand out, and stared at the mass between my fingers. Nausea and disgust crept up the cold tile walls and slowly permeated the room, as did the smell. Grabbing tissue, I wiped my hand as clean as I could, and

attempted to try again. Another wave of nausea, this time accompanied by an overwhelming feeling of entrapment amidst the stench and the isolation that seemed to be closing in. There was no escape, and certainly no walking out. Hell no, no walking out at all. Fear, sadness. This was my life now. An ugly brown mess of paralysis – physical, emotional, and spiritual brokenness. Long ago, I used to have recurring dreams about being buried alive by people who said they loved me. Now, I was in that deep, dark hole again. Only this was no nightmare. This was more real and terrifying. And I could not get out. Maybe not ever. I squeezed my gloved hand into a hard fist and pounded the wall beside me, with all the strength I had left, and erupted in an explosion of shameless tears and violent cursing. The palette of smeared feces beside me was the total despair and desolation that I had become in that moment.

"God, damn it! Why have you left me? Why? Haven't I at least tried to live a good life?" I whispered angrily, through gritted teeth.

The words, like my tears, slid out of the bleakness. Ugly, pitiful words. Weren't these words similar to what Christ had said at His own cruci-fixion? I could not stay in this purgatory, this place of rage and fear. It would be all consuming, and I knew it. What were those next words, His words? What were they? I needed to find them quickly. I knew I was slipping away.

"Father, into your hands I commend my spirit."

Yes. Those words. They came to me softly, from somewhere in my memory. In my head, I repeated them over and over, clinging to them like some psychological life raft, a mantra of sorts, and finally whispered them, in a fervent prayer, aloud. I leaned against them, letting them carry me to a safer place, back to the comfort of God. Slowly, I began to relax, to not be so terrified of whatever was coming next. I was worn out from the rage and sadness, the complete loss of dig-nity, that I had just experienced. I closed my eyes and let the fear and anger ebb and flow, until I could breathe normally again.

"It happens," I finally said aloud, smiling at the intended pun. I can find my way out of this mess, after I clean it up. I have to trust that I will be ok. No fear. Just faith. Even when going through hell.

Just keep going. Winston Churchhill had said it once, so it was good enough for me. I decided to trust God – and it was a conscious decision–no matter what. And I did eventually master the digi-stim skill. Not to be added to a resume any time, though, and no more graphic details necessary, I don't think! Trying to smile.

A Laying On of Hands

Acts 28:8 Paul went in to see him and, after prayer, placed his hands on him and healed him.

Sometime in mid-July, 2014, I remember my youngest daughter, her boyfriend, and a friend of his, coming to visit while I was in intensive rehab, and playing a game of "Cards Against Humanity" – a rather strange, but comical, card game. As sweet as they were to try to keep me entertained, my heart was not in the game, and I tried hard not to let it show. I was struggling mightily with the idea that I could potentially be a burden to my children – a lot earlier in life than the norm – and I was allowing the intrusive thoughts *to keep me from enjoying the moment. Had my daughter been by herself, or with her sister, I might have shared my feelings and had an honest discussion about my potential future in a wheelchair, and all of the complications that could develop in tandem. Instead, I tried, with minimal success, to put on the proverbial happy face and escape the mounting fear of a life of paralysis. Of course, that ended up being a bust, and, after a yeoman's effort at livening up an otherwise dismal room, the card game was packed up and my daughter and friends left. I didn't much blame them.*

I sulked, had a good cry, and stared out the window, but saw nothing. Then, I remembered it was in these moments that I needed to offer thanks for the blessings I had. My home, my children, the memories of so many fun and meaningful times, the great water oak tree in my backyard, people who loved me. Then, as if on cue, in they came, one by one, a handful of tennis friends, my sister-in-law, and one of my nieces. They brought food, adult beverages, and lots of cheer. But before the merriment could commence, they wanted to say a prayer. In an instant, the mood of the room diminished, as did the drone of hospital busyness, and they quietly gathered around my bed. Then, in one of the most loving acts I have ever had the privilege to witness, they each put their hands on my legs, bowed their heads, and closed their eyes. Ginger, the designated speaker, began reading a most eloquent prayer for my healing. Admittedly, my eyes, too, were closed, at first. But as the heartfelt prayer continued, I felt compelled to open them. Not out of irreverence or curiosity, as I innately knew, without seeing, that they were all quietly weeping, and I loved them for such selflessness. Rather, I felt it necessary for my own soul, to take in this scene, to remember it—and them—as one of the many blessings of my life. As I watched each one intently, I began to realize that I was being healed. Not physically, at least not in this moment, but emotionally and spiritually, I had received a transfusion, of sorts, and I could smile once again.

With the sincere prayers and thanksgiving offered on my behalf done, the party began. Complete with tasty snacks and beverages, and lots of funny stories exchanged, it was indeed a joyful time. I took another moment to study each of them, and to think about what the evening had meant to me. I had been revived, another chance to experience some happiness, despite the devastating situation in which I found myself. Perhaps healing – emotionally, as well as physically – would also happen slowly, and with occasional setbacks. There was no way to know for sure. But I had been saved from wallowing in despair yet again by friends who had reached out to me the best way they knew how, and it meant everything to me. As I finally closed my eyes to sleep, I smiled one more time. I could see them. And I could still feel their hands on my legs. Perhaps, they will see me move them one day soon.

The next morning, the receptionist at the front desk who delivered mail, came to my room, as she did daily, followed by my nurse for the day shift. They both smiled broadly, and stared for several minutes at the many floral arrangements and at the cards taped lovingly to the closet doors, and the prayer shawls draped across my bed and other chairs in the room.

"I declare," the receptionist said, shaking her head, "I have never seen a room fill up so with all of this love."

"You should hear what goes on in this room," the nurse said, jokingly. "All kinds of cackling and laughing, and such. I don't believe this place has ever seen this much raucousness and so many visitors."

"What does it all mean?" I said, rolling my eyes, and smiling appreciatively, as another fresh bouquet and a handful of cards were delivered to me.

"It means that you are well-loved and quite a friend," the receptionist stated simply, "and it means you are a person of good character."

"Man, I have all of you fooled, then."

I laughed heartily, but she did not. Instead, she patted my feet, and looked me squarely in the eyes.

"I don't have to know anything at all about you, except what I see in here, to know what kind of person you are." She gestured to the tokens of kindness all over the room. "All of these people didn't do all of this just to be nice. Your friends care about you and will be a great resource and *comfort to you, sweetie, just wait and see. Friends are a healing gift from heaven, I do believe."*

"Yes, they are. I'm not sure I could have ever made it this far without them."

And it was true. From tennis friends, former high school buddies, former work colleagues, camping comrades, church family, and more. There had been enough kindness shown to more than carry me through whatever might be in front of me on this journey. I remembered a scene from one of my favorite old television comedies, "The Golden Girls". Estelle Getty's character wanted to know what her friends really thought of her, so she staged her own death and quietly observed her funeral wake. Of course, antics and hilarity ensued. How fortunate for me! I got to see what I meant to my friends, and did not have to pretend I had died – though, sometimes it feels as if my world is falling apart. But my friends had been there at just the right time, and I would be eternally grateful for them all.

A Comic Interlude, Take One (Wheelchair Tips and Quips!)

Genesis 21:6 Sarah said, "God has brought me laughter, and everyone who hears about this will laugh with me".

1. *When in a wheelchair trying to pass a slower moving patient in the hall, it is possible to take out a doctor or nurse, or whomever is in the "other lane".*
2. *While operating a wheelchair, go slowly down ramps, and lean backwards – unless rolling uncontrollably and falling is your idea of fun.*
3. *If asked why you did or did not do something, just smile and say, "Because that's*

how I roll"…..then roll that wheelchair right on out of there!

4. *Power outages are so much fun in a rehab facility. Especially in an electrically operated bed. Fire alarms are exciting, too.*

5. *When being pushed in a wheelchair and rolling over the slightest bump – especially on sidewalks – hold onto something. Seriously. Refer to # 2.*

6. *In the life of those with disabilities, there develops a love/hate relationship with anything Velcro – seats, straps, equipment, braces. Learn to appreciate that ripping sound!*

7. *"I'm not gonna take that sitting down!" becomes a much more acceptable response, when spoken by one in a wheelchair.*

8. *Accepting a challenge from a young, former motorcyclist in a wheelchair to race in the hallways can be entertaining. Well, maybe not to the nurses. Channeling our inner "Days of Thunder"…*

9. *Local restaurants have some kind of aversion to delivering takeout to a rehab facility. I wonder if it could have been that bottle of wine we tried to order?*

10. *Having the reputation for being the "party girl" on the hall unit was rather fun. My motto has always been, "If you ain't livin' on the edge – then, you ain't got a view!" Why change now?*

Home Bittersweet Home

2 Corinthians 5:1 "For we know that if the earthly tent we live in is destroyed, we have a building from God, an eternal house in heaven, not built by human hands."

Going Home

*I*t was a Sunday, and I was going home for a day visit. It would be an opportunity to see how well I could execute all of the necessary skills to be home permanently. If I were successful, I would go home for good on Tuesday. If not, then arrangements would be made to extend rehabilitation. That was what I knew. What I did not know was how intensely emotional that first trip would *be. My daughters dutifully packed me into the car, after a successful transfer to the front seat, and we talked about how the day would play out. Lunch prepared by a friend, and an easy after-noon. We would discuss future arrangements, and catch up on their plans. Daughter McKenna would be returning to Rock Hill, SC, and Gracyn would soon be returning to Presbyterian College in Clinton, SC. All well and good, until we pulled into the driveway, and I saw the ramp that had been lovingly built for me by friends and family. I was the handicapped person that must have it. Immediately, I took the deepest of breaths to steady my nerves. But that was no preparation for what would come next.*

Entering the house was bittersweet and superficial, at best. But underneath was a cat-aclysmic quake of sadness and rage. This was not my dwelling. Nothing was the same. I literally saw everything from a different point of view, and stopping the tidal wave of tears was fruitless. Now, I was negotiating how to move in my own home. Can't reach this. Can't see that. My bedroom upstairs was off limits. Everything upstairs was off limits. As the downstairs bathroom remodel would take place in the near future, I had to have a portable toilet – yes, the kind one has to empty oneself – set up in the den, and it was a sorrowful reminder of the degree to which life had drastically changed. Have I mentioned those horrid adult incontinence panties? Yep, still had to have those, too, and likely would until recovery, though I had found a brand that was much less cumbersome. Because my daughters had worked tirelessly to arrange the rooms, the cabinets, the pathways in a manner that would accommodate me, I would not let myself completely enter the twilight zone, much as I felt my psyche slipping into that dark place. I adjusted the smile on my face and attempted to verbally appreciate all of the effort made on my behalf. How difficult this must have been for my girls – and how I would give anything to have spared them from having to give so much. A wave of resentment and guilt crept into my head.

This is your fault. Because of you, your girls have an invalid for a mother. You have brought this hardship on them and on everyone else who must now help you.

Cognitively, I knew that this rarity that had happened was no more my fault than the ebb and flow of tides, but worry somehow managed to whittle away at me like an eroding shoreline. I lashed back at the devilish, intrusive thoughts of loss, trying to shove them out of my way.

Stop it. Toughen up, if you love these girls. You can have some independence. Get over yourself and do whatever must be done. You are not the first person to experience extreme hardship, and many have had to endure horrors much worse than this. Enjoy the day, as others have worked to make it a good one just for you.

And so, a tasty lunch, as well as the remainder of the day, was pleasant. I kept the evilness of despair at bay, and thus enjoyed not being confined to a hospital of any kind. Plans were in the works for a walk-in shower and bench in the downstairs den bathroom, with all of the necessary accoutrements for a handicapped individual. We discussed what small modifications would be needed to allow access to my Florida room and outside deck. The decision had previously been made for me to use the den as my bedroom, and essentially, to live solely on the ground level of my house. After much debate with family, I had nixed the idea of trying to return to my master bedroom and bath upstairs, though I understood their wanting me to return to my own comfortable surroundings. Of a certainty, I also wanted that more than anything. However, having the dubious distinction of being the only member of the family who had wheelchair experience, I knew exactly what this would entail. Simply getting out of bed and then up and down stairs repeatedly, would involve an initial transfer from the bed to a wheel- chair, then from the wheelchair to the stair lift, fol- lowed by a leisurely lift ride down the stairs, only to be followed by a transfer to yet a second wheel- chair on the ground level. This cumbersome rou- tine – not to mention the necessity of wheelchairs being left flush against stairs for transfer access – would be difficult for others to navigate around, as well. In the event of an emergency, such as a fire, I would become a crispy critter before I could make it to the top of the stairs, especially if I were alone.

With this important decision being made, the girls carefully packed me and my day bag in the car, and drove back to Health South Rehabilitation Facility. After the visit home without any major catastrophes, other than the emotional turmoil, I was sure I would be allowed to come home as scheduled. As I lay awake, pondering the events of the day, and the reality that home, as well as life, would be vastly different, I chastised myself some for fretting about that which I could no longer control. I had told myself before, and others had told me as well, to allow time to grieve the loss of my legs and that part of my life – even if recovery were long-term. I knew that I had saddled myself with high expectations for a quicker recovery, because I always attempt to beat a deadline with successful completion of any task. I had attempted to steel emotions, skip over all of the tough stuff, and find a way to orchestrate my own healing on my own schedule. Going home – or to the place that once felt like my sanctuary – reminded me that nothing on *this earth is ever guaranteed to be the way we want. I knew, at least what I had always learned in Sunday School as a child, was that God had this "house in heaven" that had many rooms, and one day, if I were a good little girl, I could have some space there. Of course, mine would have the best toys and sweet animals brought to me by the best Santa Claus. Ah, childhood perception. As an adult – a mere sojourner on this path to understanding the many layers of strength and truth contained in the Bible, I was only beginning to comprehend that always being willing to allow God to work within me and through others, especially in the midst of tragedy, was "home" in the best possible way, and that I could always "live" there, as long as I drew breath. And indeed, I did get to finally leave inpatient rehabilitation, as scheduled. Of course, regular 2-3 times per week outpatient rehab would be arranged for me, once I had settled at home. I would find that adjusting would be no easy task, and one of trial and error, most often at my expense. Experience would be the most effective teacher, to be sure.*

Bathing Beauty

I was now sleeping in a hospital bed in what had been my den, though I would eventually graduate to a daybed borrowed from a friend. The adjoining bathroom would not yet accommodate my wheelchair, and the demolition and remodel was scheduled to begin soon. Thus, the biggest challenges for me would be those related to hygiene. A portable toilet – yep, same one – had to be set up beside my bed, and I had to consider how I would be able to bathe. A good friend had offered for me to come to their home, which was wheelchair accessible, to use their shower. Though the offer was sweet, the actual possibility proved to be more difficult to manage. Since I could not yet drive, I would have to schedule a ride to her home and back. My wheelchair would have to be packed up and hauled there. Not to mention the fact that I would have to learn to negotiate her shower, and inconvenience her family twice a week, at minimum.

In a streak of genius – at least, to my mind – I thought about my camping days, and all of the times I had bathed or showered in an out-door environment. Why not? I could alleviate the need for transportation, could shower any time I wanted, and the arrangement would only be for a few weeks, while the bath remodel took place. So, much to the chagrin of my girls, who only wanted me to be comfortable, the outside bath was born. When shower time was needed, the bowl part of the portable toilet was removed and an instant shower seat of sorts was created. I donned gym shorts and a T-shirt – have I men-tioned it being hard, just to get dressed? – and rolled out to my backyard deck, where one of the girls had diligently brought towels, shampoo and such, and large containers of water. As it was still a hot, southern August, I did not have to battle cold weather at all, and I found the entire experi-ence rather exhilarating. Perhaps it brought just a small bit of fun and good memories back into my life. Nurse tech Debra would be smiling, and hopefully, proud!

Thankfully, the bath remodel had also begun. Now, I am most fortunate to know many incred-ible people that I have met playing tennis over the years, largely at The Rockbridge Club. Several of the guys there were quite handy and experienced with construction and remodeling. My brother, Hank, and my former husband Chris, both also tennis players, helped to organize the effort, and the demolition was in full swing. The kitchen pantry backed up to the bathroom, which needed to be slightly enlarged to accommodate the roll-in shower and bench seat, so it was decided that the pantry would need to go. And, thus, the excitement began. Of course, being fun-loving, as well as hard-working guys that fit this task around their day jobs, required many days of tearing down, plumbing, tiling, installing new fixtures, painting, and such. During those days, the house was an overgrown jungle of boards, wires, dust, and trash. Therefore, there were more than a few cases of beer, chicken wings, and pizza to be consumed amidst the craziness, laughter, pranks, stories, and loud music. Their presence kept me focused on the remodel project, rather than on those first extremely difficult days of adjusting at home. At the end of it all, though, was one of the nicest and most functional bathrooms! To say that I was thrilled with the result would be a huge under-statement. What meant even more to me was that these folks were willing to give me their time – a lot of it – as well as their talents, as a labor of love. In addition, friends near and far organized and maintained a meal train – an online method of signing up to provide meals–during those crazy days. How very lucky I am to have such people in my life. They are more valuable than I thought possible, and I was, and will remain, thankful for each of them.

Meltdowns

My first real "thermonuclear meltdown" – besides that wretched evening in the bathroom at rehab – naturally happened at home. I don't remember exactly what was in the glass, but I do remember trying to pour liquid into it – could have been wine?–and then accidentally drop-ping it, the glass shattering immediately. What I remember vividly is the level of surprising rage that engulfed me as I quietly and helplessly watched the liquid spread across the tiled floor, like a growing disease. I remember screaming until my throat hurt, as long and as loudly as I possibly could, in an angry soliloquy to God, demanding to know why my girls and I were saddled with this atrocity. I am the mother, and I cannot be helpless! Admittedly, it felt cathartic to release all of that emotion, but I regretted that Gracyn was standing behind me, frozen only for a moment, as I unleashed the rather demonic tirade. To this day, I am not completely sure, but I think that both of my girls offered quiet comfort and stability, as they lovingly cleaned up my mess and tried to restore normalcy. My mind wandered back to times when I was a school counselor, and would sometimes sit on the floor with overly dis-traught children, who were unable to contain, or appropriately express, their explosion of emo-tion, and quietly hold them while they wore them-selves out with tears and screams. Often times, they were so spent that they could not remember some of the details of what had just happened. Now, I understood that on a much more personal level. Thankfully, the meltdowns have been few, and none quite as intense as the first one, though there have been moments of unspeakable sadness and regret.

Another such time involved my dog, Annie. Of course, I wanted to allow her to come inside the house with me, especially during a thunderstorm, or when the weather was extremely cold, as I have always done. I thought I could still manage her by myself, though I should have known better. She is such good company, and so sweet. There has always been a designated blanket-lined chair in the den that she loved to jump up in and snuggle between the armrests. This particular night was freezing, and I let her inside before I lifted myself on my daybed, also now in the den. I had hoped that she would be able to control her bowels and bladder this night, fully knowing that I was likely engaging in wishful thinking, of sorts, and I was right. Upon waking the next morning at dawn, when the house was still relatively dark, I was horrified to find that she had not only urinated in the house, but also defecated all over the den. I got myself into my chair and made an attempt to get around the land mines toward the door to let her out, when I discovered that I had rolled through a large portion of the mess she had made. It was more than I could withstand. The tears came quickly, though at least there was no screaming involved, this time. I got myself back in bed and called my friend Julie, who lived close by.

Julie came over as quickly as I called, dutifully let Annie outside, and then began cleaning up the wretched mess. There was great weeping and wailing and gnashing of teeth, as I lamented the rather frustrating start to the morning. When I realized Julie was kneeling beside my wheelchair, and trying to clean the tread of the tires with a toothpick, the ridiculousness of the situation became humorously evident, and I burst into fits of laughter.

"Now, you're laughing?" She looked at me incredulously, holding up the toothpick, which made me howl even more.

"Good lord, Julie, I can't even believe this," I gasped for breath and tried not to laugh further, but that was futile.

"YOU can't believe it?" She hollered, and shook the toothpick. "What the hell, I'm cleaning dog doo out of a damn wheelchair, and it's still

not even 8:00 o'clock in the morning! You know you're a good friend, when I do that!"

"You know what," I quickly offered, "just roll the thing into my shower and hose that bad boy down with the hand-held shower head. It'll be much easier. And I owe you, big time!" I smiled, but was careful not to laugh.

"You know you are going to have to make arrangements to have Annie stay elsewhere, at least while the weather is this cold, right? I mean, I know you love her, but, Pat, this is not fair to you to try to keep her here. You can't do it all in a wheelchair!" Julie kept talking, as she finished the task of cleaning up my den.

Of course, I knew that she was right, but it was incredibly hard to let go of that task, as I had to do for many others. The inevitable truth was that I had to give up control of many things in my life, and that reality was sobering for me. With great reluctance, I had to ask my girls and their dad to help me figure out a solution. Sadly, that also added guilt to my already-burgeoning supply of negativity, and I cried again, but agreed that Annie going to temporarily live with my ex was, indeed, the best solution. Admittedly, I could have avoided that disaster, had I not been so determined to try to go about business as usual.

The Little Red Machine

One of the hardest dilemmas for me to face has been the loss of my ability to drive my beloved little car. There are some days that I look longingly at the sleek, little red sportster that sits in my now electronically accessible garage, and smile. Sometimes I actually say, "I can't wait to drive you again". Then, there are some days when I pass by it, that I reach out to touch the door handle and just cry, wishing I could feel the pedals move beneath my feet, and the stick shift slide through the gears. I long to stand to sing and play my guitar, play a game of tennis, walk down the beach one day with my girls, and perhaps one day, run behind a grandchild trying to catch crabs on the beach at night. Sometimes, especially when I am alone, I have to remember to take heart in the things I can still do, not get lost in the things I cannot – and believe that recovery is still possible. A long, hard road it will be, but worth all of the tears, meltdowns, and hard work that are in front of me. I still visualize myself in that car.

Dad

I was greatly blessed, in those early days at home, with a most important life lesson from my father, a former POW during World War II, and not one to have emotional displays of any kind. He worked hard to get himself in college after the war, via the G.I. bill, and as a result, he instilled in me the value and privilege of education. I remember his being so delighted with an internet discovery I found – that our family motto was, "Capta majora" – a Latin phrase, meaning "Seek Greater Things". I think he still tries hard to live that in many ways, despite his own deteriorating physical condition. While he never openly expressed any sadness at my having to be in a wheelchair, I knew it hurt him immensely to see me in a state of physical disability. I could see everything he did not say in his eyes. It must have been hard for him to see his child facing such a devastating condition, especially at my relatively young age of almost 60. I know it would be unbearable for me to see my children have to face such, at any age.

One day, while the demolition of the bathroom was taking place, he came to my house, weaving his walker around all of the mess, and joking with my brothers and the work crew, and then stood quietly beside me at the kitchen counter.

"Patricia," he said without a smile, "here is a little something to help with expenses. I know they must be mounting by now."

With that, he pushed what was most certainly a folded check across the counter toward me. It was a similar scenario I had experienced before with very special friends, who had also freely donated money on my behalf. Then, as well as now, the tears came freely and I was overwhelmed with the caring generosity, and thanked him profusely, while squeezing his hand. But his reaction was different from most. He never smiled, never flinched, or even expressed a word of sympathy. He stood for a minute, his eyes staring out the window past the grand oak tree in my backyard. What was he thinking? And then he spoke softly, still not looking directly at me.

"One should never feel sorry for oneself. Ever. It does no good."

With that, he turned and headed for the front door, waving to all and saying his goodbyes. At first, I was hurt. I never even got a hug. Why was he so distant like that, especially now? For a few moments, I sulked.

I do not feel sorry for myself! I was just feeling grateful for the caring generosity!

But as the day wore on – along with my thoughts about what he had said and done – I began to fathom the depths of the man. Having grown up with few advantages and secretly joining the military at the age of 15, as many did during those times, and then becoming a POW at the tender age of 19, he experienced the horrors of war and the tougher side of life, when most that age were having fun at their high school proms and going to football games. Perhaps I would have learned to steel my emotions as well, had I been forced to grow up as quickly as he had, having experienced what it was like to be shot and captured as a prisoner. He had been required to become a man far before he should have. I began to understand, in a small way, a measure of why he is often so stoic. In that moment, I wished I could have given him some of those wonder years back.

More importantly, I began to realize that his seemingly stern response was not the scolding that I believed it to be, but rather an act of deepest love. He had learned to survive the atrocities of war by not ever allowing himself to express self-pity. As hard as it was for him to see me in this debilitating condition, he knew that my survival and recovery would depend largely on my willingness to never give up – and that no one could do the hard work but me. Interestingly, my dad has repeatedly told me, since my injury, that he loves me, and that he prays for my recovery often. It seems that we both believe that my healing will require not only hard work, but divine work, as well. I actually searched in the Bible for relevant texts about the way my father had responded to my paralysis. I found one such text that exemplified in a way I was not expecting. The simplicity speaks for itself:

Proverbs 27: 5-6 "Better is open rebuke than hidden love. Wounds from a friend can be trusted, but an enemy multiplies kisses."

Back to Work

I made the decision to go back to my part-time job as a counselor at The Carolina Children's Home Child and Adult Outpatient Counseling Center within a week of being home. In retrospect, I likely was not physically ready to return to work so quickly, as I actually fell out of my chair on the first day, while in the bathroom there, but I had felt trapped in the house for the better part of a month, without being able to drive, or even to ride in some models of vehicles. Going back to the center, and immersing myself in the needs of others, was so much more therapeutic than I could have ever imagined. Not sure who ben-efitted more – me, or my clients. Thanks to my friend Kat, the office manager there, who gra-ciously offered to transport me until I had my own transportation, I was able to resume a vital part of my life, and feel useful once again. I credit my time there with helping me to heal, emotionally, and to find a renewed sense of purpose in my new life at home. When it was announced, in mid September of 2015, that the entire facility would close, I was crushed. What would I do without this amazing place? I had done volunteer work there, as a young adult, and the Home had been a part of the Columbia community since before I was born. Saying goodbye to clients, to that part of my life, was a difficult and tremendous loss, leaving me emotionally void for the better part of a week.

Friends

Since being home, several people have asked about friends. They want to know if mine are standing by me, if any of them disappeared after I became disabled. Have there been any surprises? I found it odd, in a way, that the topic of friends would even be on the radar of anyone – but then, no one that is doing the asking has ever been in my particular situation before. The short answer is yes – and no. I will answer the "no" part first. None of my friends have done anything that I found out of character, or strange. None of my close friends have deserted me in any way, whatsoever. Many have absolutely rocked my world with the amount of kindness and concern that they have shown. I do not know what I would do without the weekly consistency of friends Julie, Kat, Alicia, and Elaine. Barbara has sent a card almost monthly, it seems. My friend Nancy from Louisiana, who jumped on a plane to visit, healed me in ways I did not think possible. Some brought me to tears with their generosity. My friends are legion. I cannot even count the number of those who visited, called, brought meals, or dropped by to see me. Were there people who did not come around after I became disabled? Perhaps one or two; but, in fairness, we do not always know the nuances of the life of another. Far be it from me to judge. Besides, no one can improve his or her lot in life, if time is spent fretting over what one thinks another did, or did not do. This journey is mine to make of it what I will. My friends have made that journey easier to bear, and I am so blessed to have every single one.

Beer Cheer

After a particularly fun gathering at the house, of daughters McKenna and Gracyn, brothers Erick and Hank, sister-in-law Monica, nieces Allie and Dorothy, and Dad and wife, Kaye, I found myself looking at a styrofoam cooler of leftover beer that was on the floor in the kitchen. The ice was already half melted and the beer needed to go in the refrigerator. What to do? Lifting the cooler was not possible for me.

Think, Pat, think. Too much for one person to drink, although the idea is not altogether bad. Call a friend or two for an impromptu party? Too early in the morning, and this needs to be handled now. OK, kiddo, time to amp up the brainpower and get creative.

Taking the lid off the cooler, and turning it upside down so that it was more like a tray with a grooved edge, I placed it on my lap. Each bottle of beer was then carefully arranged on top in a way that made transporting to the refriger- ator much easier. Now, the cooler still remained almost three-quarters full with a mixture of ice and water. Lifting also remained an elusive impossibility. But I was up for the challenge! Grabbing a large plastic pitcher from a bottom cabinet, I made four or five trips to the sink, with the carefully balanced pitcher of water wedged tightly between my thighs. At last, the cooler contained a manageable level of contents for my next thrilling act. Rolling my chair and foot piece up against one of the broad sides of the cooler, I pushed and maneuvered it out of the kitchen and through the hallway to the front door. After locking my chair into position, I reached down and tipped the cooler forward, past the open door, until the water spilled out, spreading over the front porch and onto the front lawn.

I hope none of my neighbors drive by while I'm doing this. Oh look, there's that lady neighbor that always looks mad, out for her morning walk. She definitely looks mad today. Yeah, hi. Please don't ask. Closing the door, now, bye! Whew! I am woman, hear me roar, right?

Now, that was what I call a confidence builder!

A Concert of Prayer

James 5:14-15 "Is anyone among you sick? Let them call the elders of the church to pray over them with oil in the name of the Lord. And the prayer offered in faith will make the sick person well; the Lord will raise them up."

In mid-August, shortly after I came home from inpatient rehab at Health South, the priest and parish members of my church organized a concert of prayer for me, and for the needs of any who wished special prayers for healing. An Episcopal church, St. Michael and All Angels has always been a unique parish, made up of uncommonly caring and committed folk who never fail to come together in time of need. As in any family or organization, our church has also faced both prosperous times, and times of great trial. But always, the people here give unceasingly, and find ways to come together in love. No fair weather friends are these; strong and real people who have weathered much in their own lives. I count myself most fortunate to belong to this community of worship.

A concert of prayer is a quiet and meaningful service, consisting primarily of very focused prayer and contemplative music. People pray individually and collectively for specific needs of healing, and offer thanks to God for hearing these prayers and praise. Many were invited to this service – and many were in attendance, even the tennis team on which my niece plays. So many, in fact, that it took longer than expected for one priest to hear all of the requests for healing prayer, as oil was administered to foreheads in a symbolic gesture of forgiving and redemptive love. I do not think we have ever had a service quite like this one. I sat in the back of the church, with our Praise Choir, anchored in my wheelchair, guitar in hand, and happy to be seated where a private moment of tears was less obvious. I was also afforded a unique view of people as they entered the church, and I was greatly moved by family, acquaintances, former colleagues, and friends alike that had gathered together, largely on my behalf. Several stopped to hold my hand, give me a hug, or just to smile warmly as they entered the sanctuary. I found myself praying for them, as well.

As this beautiful service continued, I became more acutely aware of my own need for healing. Physically, of course, but perhaps spiritually, even more so. My life had taken such a horrific and sudden turn, that I was ill prepared for the onslaught of emotion and anxiety over the unknown that had invaded my world. I was painfully aware that, in the end, I had to endure my tragedy. No one else could do this, but me. The journey was mine, alone. Suddenly, my thoughts flashed back to that wretched night in the rehab facility, when I had attempted digital stimulation, and to my first meltdown, when I had helplessly watched as liquid and broken glass spread across the floor. Instantly, a host of negativity played out, intrusively, in my thoughts.

"You're alone," it whispered, "and you will never be the same."

"But I am here, and in this place," an inner voice whispered softly, " and I have promised that I am with you, always."

I looked around the church at the people gathered here to worship. My friends, all, every one of them making an effort to be Christ to me, in their own way. Then, the words of a piece of taize music that we had just sung, began to sing themselves, quietly in my head:

"Bless the Lord, my soul; and bless God's holy name. Bless the Lord, my soul, who leads me into life."

This was now my journey, hard or no. I was glad these people were all here in this church. Because of them, at least it would be easier to go the distance. They are all gifts from God. When I would return to play and sing for one of our regular, monthly contemporary services, the Praise Choir would sit in the choir stalls in the front of the church, instead of where we had been seated in *the back, for this service. There is no ramp up there, and the alter area is not designed for such. I was keenly aware that a few able-bodied individuals would have to lift me, in my chair up and down for a service, and that I would be a bit on display. While I was not looking forward to that part of returning to church, I knew that this, too, would pass. Realistically, once the newness of the situation had worn off, I would get back to the business of everyday living. Sadly, that would be without my legs for a very long time. But it was all part of the recovery process, so I would learn to live in this manner, for as long as I must.*

Hopkins Heroes

Romans 12:12 *"Be joyful in hope, patient in affliction, faithful in prayer."*

I n mid-September, after the hectic remodel of the bathroom, I began to focus once again on what might be a more definitive diagnosis. Dr. Petit had indicated that he thought something else besides transverse myelitis might be going on, and I had contemplated what a next step might be to find an answer. It did not take long to begin making plans to travel to Johns Hopkins Hospital in Baltimore, Maryland. One of my high school friends, Susan, who was from Baltimore, had adamantly insisted that Hopkins was the place for me. As I researched hospitals both near *and far, and began narrowing the field of possibilities, it did indeed appear as if this facility would be a very good fit for my needs. As fortune would have it, Johns Hopkins was the only hospital in the country with a transverse myelitis clinic, and therefore, best able to determine if that would be the final diagnosis. With a flurry of paperwork, phone calls, and records exchanged, I was accepted as a patient, and the trip was planned. While both of my daughters offered to make the trip with me, I did not want to take McKenna away from her first big job for an extended period of time, nor Gracyn, from her last year in college. I might need them to make another trip with me, depending on this outcome. So, who would drive for this extended road trip?*

Raenell, the sister of my good friend Charlene, is tall, with closely cropped blonde hair, feisty, and as colorful as she is kind. A retired nurse, living in the eastern part of the state, Raenell was well known for her love of adventurous travel, and was unafraid to venture anywhere on her own. She would be the perfect travel companion and driver, since I would have to learn to drive with hand-held controls, and arrange for a properly outfitted car before I would be allowed to drive myself. But would she agree to go, even with me paying the way? It was a huge demand of time and energy. I made a quick call to her.

"Well, damn right, I'll go! Baltimore in Autumn, Maryland crab cakes, an adult beverage or two, and a trip with you to find some answers? You bet, let's do it!"

Raenell could not have been more gracious, or sound more willing to help in this manner. With hotel reservations made, an itinerary planned, my wheelchair packed in the trunk of her car, and a cooler full of snacks and drinks, we rolled down I-77, headed north, a variety of light classic rock music playing, in the Monday morning hours of mid-October. Raenell regaled me with tales of previous trips, her nursing days, and caught me up on all family activity. For lunch, we stopped for a wonderful rest area picnic break, then drove to Roanoke, Virginia to spend the night. While we likely could have driven the entire way to Baltimore in the one day, I had not been sure about how travel would impact me physically, and did not want to wear Raenell out, as she would have to shoulder all of the driving, so I had made the decision to spend the night, then set out the next day for the duration of the trip. The result was a leisurely, relaxed drive, with no pressure to be anywhere by a specific time, and I was so glad that it had been planned as such.

The lightheartedness of the trip, and our constant chatter about everything except my paralysis, kept me in a positive frame of mind, free from stressful worry. It was exhilarating to be on the road, seeing the country again, and enjoying new and interesting sights. Driving across the Chesapeake Bay – except for the tunnel, which is an engineering wonder, but has never done anything for my claustrophobia–and into Baltimore under deep blue and clear skies gave me pause to be thankful for sun glistening on beautiful water. It imparted a sense of tranquility that I knew was very much needed, so I took a moment to revel in the scenery, then began to look for our hotel, via the phone GPS system. There was definitely a new appreciation for the nuances of modern technology, as we arrived at our destination with no complications. Once inside our room, we unpacked, stretched our legs (well, kind of!) and enjoyed a small glass of wine and made plans for dinner and locating the neurology area of the hospital for the next morning appointment.

Without hesitation, the bay area was chosen for our early evening meal, largely for the ambience, and we decided to ride around a bit to see what struck our fancy. As the idea was to go for local color, so to speak, we did not want a chain restaurant, but rather one that appeared seasoned and fun. It did not take long to find what we wanted.

"There, that's it right there, check that out!" I giggled excitedly.

Motioning for Raenell to begin looking for a place to park, we instantly agreed on a seafood restaurant and bar directly across from the water. A light blue, long rectangular shaped board was stretched across the entire front of the place, with white painted letters that said, "Riptide By the Bay". With a quaint and inviting exterior, the front was primarily glass, with stained wooden double doors that were propped open, and a sprinkling of wrought iron tables and chairs arranged al fresco on the old brick sidewalk. There was a large plastic jack o' lantern hanging in the window, on the right side of the door, along with advertisements about an upcoming Halloween bash. A few soft green and leafy plants on either side of the door gave an air of contemporary coolness. Since there was a decent step up to the inside of the establishment, we opted for outside dining, which we likely would have done, regardless. Almost immediately, a waiter came for a drink order. We guessed him to be the manager, as he seemed a bit older than the average wait staff, though he was similarly dressed in casual knee-length shorts, flip flops, and a long-sleeved, button down white shirt that was rolled in a three-quarter length. Running his fingers through hair that was tousled and graying ever so slightly at the temple, he smiled affably and his ingenuous manner was instantly endearing.

"Well, ladies, I bet I can get you something phenomenal to drink, huh?" He placed his hands decisively on his hips. His accent betrayed a bit of perhaps Boston, we decided.

"Well, what do y'all have?" I smiled back at him.

"Oh, oh no, wait! Y'all?" He grinned even more. "Hey!" he hollered loudly to whoever was inside, "I do believe we have some gen-oo-wine southern belles here, folks!"

I put forth my best Scarlett O'Hara drawl, and feigned slight displeasure.

"Why, I'm not sure of your intentions, sir! My daddy, the general, warned me about such crassness from… pausing for effect…Yankees!" I looked at him disdainfully, while he and a few other patrons laughed aloud. Raenell and I knew we had found the right place.

"Oh, oh, oh, here we go," he said, eyes sparkling, as he dragged up one of the wrought iron chairs and sat casually between us, propping his elbows on the table and his face against his hands. "Seriously, where are you from?"

And so we chatted briefly with Mike about South Carolina, why we were in the area, and about Baltimore in general. He explained that the old detective show, "Homicide, Life on the Streets" was filmed in the historic building directly across the way from our seats. Intermittently, he would stop by our table to ask another question about what had happened to me, and bring a fresh drink – beer for me, wine for Raenell, or a slew of oysters, shrimp, crab cakes, and more. As we were winding down with our seafood meal, Mike slid up to our table once more.

"So, you want to try a shot?" His ebullient smile revealed the prankster in his personality.

"A shot of what?" I asked innocently, while raising my eyebrows, which sent him into fits of laughter. He seemed to be quite the entertainer and became more accommodating, the more we engaged him.

"I'll be right back!" he motioned for us to remain seated, and scurried back inside.

When he returned, there were shot glasses filled with what appeared to be cinnamon schnapps, or fireballs. We expounded on the joys of such, especially in the cool Baltimore weather, and Mike eventually brought out another round. By the end of the evening, he was warmly giving us most sincere and heartfelt wishes for a successful visit to Johns Hopkins, and we were certain that our bill did not reflect all that we had ordered, or that had been given to us.

"Not bad, for a Yankee!" I called back to him.

We both laughed long and loudly, as Raenell rolled me back to the car. The wind had begun to pick up, now, and it made my wheelchair ride across the cobblestone street and walkway quite uncomfortable. I realized I was holding on to the handles of the wheelchair to keep from falling out, as the wind rocked my chair in a lateral motion, as Raenell fought for control of direction.

Perhaps I should take a moment to expound on a specific detail in this rather humorous happening. I can say, with certainty, that I am blessed in many ways. However, when the genes for big, plentiful, thick hair were being disseminated, I was left woefully lacking. Alas, my poor little head is barely covered with the thinnest of hair. Dries pretty quickly, though. But, I digress. As fate would have it, I had my hair fixed in one of those chic little messy buns that look elegant, yet effortless. The end result was supposed to be a masterful blend of casual and sophisticated. However, in order to achieve that type of perfection with my hair, assistance–in the form of one of those fake hair scrunchies–was necessary. I had spent hours looking in stores for the right texture and color, to create the most natural look. In fact, many of my friends had seen me wear my new mother's-little-helper, and profusely complimented my hairstyle, being totally unaware of my haute couture secret. Today, I had been wearing it proudly!

Back to the story.

Raenell, and I were attempting to push our way through what is now most likely a gale-force wind, as we approached a pair of colorful street musicians, long hair weaved in a Rastafarian manner, and their music, an artful blend of reggae and funk, with guitar and harmonica. They sat on the corner of one of the busiest streets in the bay area, and seemed oblivious both to the howling wind, and to us, while we battled to remain upright. As we rolled along until we hit one particularly deep crevice in the cobblestone, my chair tipped to the right, and I made a sharp counterbalance move to the left. In doing so, we managed to keep me in the chair, and avert a major accident. However, my lovely faux hair bun became instant collateral damage, as it went careening through the air to land in the middle of the street. It looked like the tail of an auburn-colored squirrel, rolled up tightly and bouncing down the road. Raenell had the full screen view of the disaster, and she began to laugh hysterically, to the point of having to gasp for breath. When I realized what had happened, I saw the extreme humor in the situation and began to laugh uncontrollably, as well. The musicians and passersby alike must have been thoroughly entertained with the two of us fighting the wind, screaming with laughter, and rolling, as fast as we could go down the street, to retrieve the wayward hair piece.

"Go, go, go!" I fought to get the words out between fits of laughter. "I'm holding on, but if I fall out and get hurt, just take me to Johns Hopkins – that way, I'll be there in the morning, anyway!"

Raenell cackled even more and instructed me to put the locks on my chair, as she chased the wayward hairpiece just past the gawking musicians, who were now right beside me.

"Hey, how's it going?" I tried to ask nonchalantly, while readjusting my newly disheveled ponytail.

Both musicians nodded approvingly, never stopping to play, as their own hair blew fiercely in the wind, but watching us with great curiosity.

"Girl," Raenell giggled as she shoved the now frazzled hairpiece in my hand, while we made our way down the street. "I gotta tell ya – the craziest things seem to happen to you!" Go figure, right?

We both laughed even more, as we sat for a few minutes in the car, and tried to compose ourselves. The comical distraction was just what I needed before the big day tomorrow. Though I was more nervous than I was willing to admit, it had been cathartic to laugh so heartily. Before going back to the hotel, we decided to ride around Baltimore in general, and Johns Hopkins, in particular, to locate the address I had been given and to find the best parking areas. Indeed, both the hospital and the university displayed prominently in downtown Baltimore, and presented – at least to this visitor – with an air of distinguished learning and excellence. I felt encouraged, though I was tentative in expressing it. I really had no idea what to expect, in terms of how doctors here might help. All I knew was that they had a reputation for being the best–and only–facility specializing in the area of my current diagnosis, and that they had examined my records and images, and were willing to see me, despite the many requests that they get from patients all over the world. Tonight, I would take comfort in knowing that some of the best doctors in the world would see me, and let tomorrow take care of itself. I fell asleep somewhere between my thanksgiving for a nice day and prayers for a hopeful outcome.

The 9:00 A.M. Wednesday morning appointment time meant that Raenell and I were up early, had a filling breakfast in the hotel lobby café, and took our coffee and juice to go. If all went as planned, I would have a solid course of action for this dreadfulness, and we would be on the road home by early afternoon. At least, that was the plan we had originally been given by our hospital concierge. Who knew hospitals had those, by the way? A rather unique concept, but efficient, I had supposed when my designated concierge had initially phoned me. Theoretically, they answered any questions, provided all necessary paperwork and communication prior to the actual hospital visit, and generally made the whole experience run more smoothly. So far, so good for us, as we had adequately navigated the correct parking garage, made it easily into the neurology wing of the building, and were still smiling, as we rubbed in the hand sanitizer given to all upon building entry.

"Patricia Brandon?"

A man's voice, with a Spanish accent, called out precisely at 9:03, in a softly raised attempt to break through the drone of waiting room patients. Assuming him to be an attendant in his starched white coat, I waved, and began to wheel slowly in his direction. A slender, quiet, and unassuming man, with dark, but graying hair, smiled pleasantly through black studious-looking glasses.

"I am Carlos Pardo-Villamizar, but most people here call me Dr. Pardo."

He smiled warmly and shook my hand. Instantly, I recognized the name of the head of the Johns Hopkins Transverse Myelitis Clinic. Before I could respond with surprise at a doctor coming to escort a patient back to an examination room, he had casually stepped behind my chair and placed his hands on the handles.

"I hope you do not mind that I push you. I thought we could get acquainted while I take you back to meet with our team."

Team? There was a team? For me? (OK, yes, I was duly impressed.)

Once in the examination room, Dr. Pardo, in his delightful Colombian accent, as I had come to know it, introduced Raenell and I to two other, perhaps younger, physicians, as well as a senior physical therapist from The Kennedy Krieger Institute across the street, and began to explain the nuances of my case.

"We do not believe that you have transverse myelitis, primarily due to the rapid onset of symptoms and paralysis. This is very rare, what you have. Let me show you more, and then I would like for you to tell us again about what you said in your letter to us about your experiences the day before the paralysis."

Raenell and I stared at each other for a moment. These doctors had actually taken the time to read what I had sent in my patient info packet, when others had completely disregarded the information as being even remotely significant. We both listened attentively, as Dr. Pardo, with a click of his computer keyboard, displayed images of my spine on a larger screen, both normal and cross-sectional views, and attempted to explain what it all meant.

"You can see this whiteness here, and in the cross-sectional view here at the T-10 level of your spine. We think it is more indicative of a vascular myelopathy, similar to a mini-stroke of sorts, in the spinal cord, rather than transverse myelitis, which usually presents with much less rapidity than what you experienced. But in order for us to be sure, we agree that we want to do a procedure called a spinal angiogram, that is the gold standard for determining such spinal cord issues. We happen to have the number one doctor in the world for this procedure right here in our hospital. If you will give us the day to procure the proper authorization with insurance and to clear the schedule of the doctor who will perform the spinal angiography, we will make arrangements to do this for you on Friday and give you more

definitive information about this condition of yours. Can you stay in Baltimore until Saturday?"

Without hesitation, Raenell spoke up and assured him that we would stay. With technicalities out of the way, Dr. Pardo had me recount the entire story to the team about lifting the garage door and feeling an unusual tiny popping sensation in my lower back. They then left the room for several minutes. When they returned, Dr. Pardo explained what their unanimous thoughts were about what might have happened.

"We believe that when you lifted your garage door, as you have done so repeatedly over time, I know, that a blood vessel in your spine became pinched, or kinked like a garden hose," *Dr. Pardo animatedly compressed his fingers to demonstrate, "and when that happened, blood – and therefore vital oxygen – was cut off from your spine. Everything below that injury would no longer function properly. Thus, you became paralyzed below the T-10 level. When we do the spinal angiogram, we may find out so much more about what is going on, and there are many possibilities."*

With that, he comfortably retreated to his world of medical terminology and spoke quickly and excitedly about the wonders of vascular malformations, dural arteriovenous fistulas, arteriovenous malformations, and a host of other medical speak terms that reminded me of his dedication and prowess as a skilled physician. But there was a passion in his voice, an unmistakable desire to help, that made the overflow of medical speak seem very assuring. He concluded with a promise that they would take care of me and go into more detail on Friday. There would be only a mild sedative, as I would need to be alert during the two-hour procedure, and take an active role in helping with the process. At the thought of assisting the number one spinal angiography doctor in the world with a medical procedure, I had to smile. Once final arrangements had been made, all forms completed, and necessary information gathered, we made our way back to the parking garage.

"How do you feel about all of this?" Raenell finally asked, as we buckled ourselves in for the ride back to the hotel.

"Well," I stopped for a moment to take in all that had just happened. "I guess this means we need to entertain ourselves for another day and find some more fun places to eat and drink, as well as plan some sightseeing. I understand that Edgar Allen Poe is buried here, and I would like to drive by the Baltimore Ravens Stadium. You know, just cruise through Baltimore, now that we have a little more time."

We both laughed and agreed we were up to all of these tasks, as we drove leisurely through the city back to the hotel. Raenell asked me once again how I felt about the upcoming procedure. Such a caring and good friend! I thought about those true feelings and decided to say aloud what was actually in my head.

"I'm ok. Nervous. A bit scared. Yeah, more than a bit scared. But I came for answers, and answers I shall have. I'm thankful for that, just to be able to be here in this place. You know, to have the opportunity for the kind of care that I have already received. I wish hospitals everywhere were this efficient and well staffed. But hey, let's

make those room arrangements, sit for a few minutes, and see what else we want to do."

Thursday, the afternoon before the spinal angiogram procedure, came much sooner than I anticipated. Whether that was because the day had been filled with cruising through downtown Baltimore, despite the misting rain, and having fun, or because I knew that worrying would just cause unnecessary discomfort – and I had enough of that – I felt an odd sort of peace. I had read, in one of my devotionals, that I should "be joyful in hope, patient in affliction, and faithful in prayer". Anytime that day when an intrusive, worrisome idea began to weave its way into my thoughts, I reminded myself of what I had read, and took a minute to reclaim those words for myself. I thought about a former young colleague of mine, who used to jokingly say, whenever she needed to gather herself in a frustrating situation, "Jesus, take the wheel!" I smiled. This time, Jesus would literally have to drive, since I certainly could not. I wonder if He would have enjoyed my little red car as much as I did? The image of me and Him, driving through winding roads, top down, laughing, with our hair whirling in the wind, made me smile even more.

Because the procedure was scheduled for Friday morning, Raenell and I decided to eat an early dinner, and spend the evening relaxing, and watching television. We meandered along the bay area again, and found a restaurant on the water, with nice views of the harbor, ships, and the shoreline. Though it did not have the quaint ambience of "Riptide", there was a similar menu and we were both hungry, as we had only noshed on a light snack for lunch. Of course, the requisite seafood and beverages were procured, and we were happy to finally get out of the car and relax. There were T-shirts hanging on the walls, proudly displaying everything local, and we could not help but notice one, in particular, that simply said, "Bawlmer". Of course, we had to ask.

"Ah, yes," our young waiter graciously explained, "It is what comes out of the mouths of locals when they've had a bit too much to drink. Instead of saying, 'Baltimore' – well, it comes out as, 'Bawlmer'."

So now, we were in the know. I think Raenell may have bought one. With the light rain still continuing, we made our way carefully back to the car, and then, the hotel, where, thankfully, the rain was beginning to dissipate. Tomorrow was supposed to be beautiful and clear. I remember going to bed that night, after some marathon "Law and Order, SVU" viewing, and hoping the positive weather prediction was a good omen. Closing my eyes, I once again pushed away intrusive thoughts.

"Jesus loves me, this I know…"

I began to mentally hum, as I traveled back (ok, way back!) to my kindergarten years, spent at St. Michael and All Angels Episcopal Church – where I still attend today, as an adult. The memory was vivid. It was my turn to be the crucifer for our morning chapel, and I was decked out in one of my favorite outfits–a dark green dress with puffed sleeves, and socks with ruffles that peeked out above lace-up saddle oxfords. My long hair was neatly braided into two lovely strands that would have made Pocahontas jealous. We sang "Jesus Loves Me" as part of the chapel service, as I carefully carried the cross. After lunch, we took our usual naps, spread out on the floor with our little mats. While I was snoozing soundly, one of the boys, whose name was Francis, had unraveled both of my braids, much to my horror, when I awoke. But I remember the teacher, Ms. Manette, having the kids sit in a circle while she artfully re-braided my hair, and turned the whole sordid affair into a learning experience.

"You know," she said lovingly, while slowly platting and smiling, "God works this way, too. When things unravel and seem like they can't be fixed, He can weave things right back together. It may not be the same. It might even be better. But God is always there, because He loves us."

I think I actually slept well and awoke feeling refreshed, but cautiously optimistic, with prayers for the doctors involved to have extremely skilled hands on this day! We dressed as quickly as we could and made our way to the main hospital building. It was already bustling with efficiency, and we were quickly escorted to a preparation area. I chose to have Raenell remain with me as long as hospital protocol would allow her to be there. I donned the necessary medical gown, had vitals checked, chatted aimlessly with nurses, and was told that the doctors involved with the procedure would come to speak with me before I was taken to the angiography room.

Swiss Dr. Gailloud (pronounced "guy-you"), the physician that would perform the spinal angiography, was tall, very European looking, with gray hair that lightly brushed over his collar. His accent was pleasing and his smile, relaxed. He introduced Italian Dr. Orzu, (I called him "Doc Orzo"!) and said that American Dr. Eckhardt would also join them in the procedure. With great detail, he explained what would happen during the two-hour ordeal.

"First, we will insert a rather large catheter in your femoral artery. Then, we will slowly examine, and take pictures of, your entire spinal cord vascular system. This will allow us to see exactly what has happened, and may give us some insight into any further procedure that might need to be done. We might even be able to determine the extent of the damage and tell you if this is likely permanent."

His words hit instantly, like a bullet that I could not dodge. Was it now possible to know – today– whether I would ever walk again? This time, I did not even attempt to stop the tears. They were autonomic, beyond my control. I knew that these doctors would think I was an emotional wreck, and call a nurse in to deal with me. But Dr. Gailloud took a step forward, and very gently held my left hand, while Dr. Orzu held my right. Raenell sat quietly, and touched my arm.

"Pat," Dr. Gailloud said lovingly, "I did not mean to upset you. I know you are going through a very difficult and frightening ordeal. I just want to give you the most information we can. We will do this together, you and I, and we will hope for the best. It will be ok. I need you to help me through this procedure."

I thanked them both for being understanding, for recognizing my fear, and explained that I just had not been ready to give up hope in that moment.

"No," Dr. Gailloud said softly. "We never give up hope, no matter what. Are you ready to do this?"

"Let's roll," I said, trying to smile, "and when do I get that nice mild sedative?"

Both doctors smiled, and assured me that we were ready to begin. Raenell was given instructions to find a specific waiting area, and given my patient identification number. This waiting room would be outfitted with a high-tech screen that displayed patient numbers, with the start times for whatever procedure was being done, and the ability to monitor how far along each patient was in their respective procedures. This way, she could grab a snack, shop in the gift area, or walk around the facility. To say that we were amazed with everything about Johns Hopkins would be a definite understatement. She made her way to the waiting room. I was administered the necessary sedative, and then escorted through a maze of corridors, by two aides, to the spinal angiography room. I said a quick and silent prayer for healing and strength.

Surprisingly, the room was an odd geometric shape that most closely resembled a diamond, and was quite large and cheerful, with huge windows that let in massive amounts of sunlight. I was transferred onto a large white table with a pillow under my head, and a much smaller one under my knees. There was a TV monitor attached to the procedure table close to my left elbow, and turned at an angle for the doctors to see, though I had a partial view of the action. A small portable table, to the right of my feet, held a myriad of surgical instruments. Interestingly, there were large dry erase boards across the wall that was opposite the windows. A few medical personnel moved about the room, making small adjustments in the TV angle, and placing a small screen just below my stomach, so that it blocked vision of my legs. When Dr. Gailloud entered the room, looking scrubbed and ready, the attending physicians both snapped in place, and I could tell that they were about to begin the spinal angio-gram procedure.

"How's my girl?" Dr. Gailloud patted my right leg lovingly, and smiled warmly.

"Ready to rock and roll," I smiled back at him. "And, by the way, I can feel you touching me, you know, right? Don't get any ideas. But the bigger question is, 'How's my doctor"?

With that, he laughed heartily, leaned toward me, and whispered, "I did sleep at a Holiday Inn last night."

Instantly, I was at ease, as the world's number one spinal angiographer went into full-blown medical mode, instructing assistants, and reminding me of the ensuing process.

"We will insert a catheter into the femoral artery, and then work our way up the spine, exploring and taking pictures, as the injected contrast will help us more accurately view the vessels in your spine. Now, Pat, when we tell you not to breathe and not to move, it is imperative that you remain completely still, do you understand? We will tell you when it is alright to breathe and move once again."

"Let me get this straight. You don't want a paraplegic to move her legs?" I rolled my eyes at him. "Gimme something difficult to do, please."

Dr. Gailloud shook his head, grinning. "There's one in every crowd. I think we found ours. And no, I don't want you to move anything. OK, Miss Pat, let's go to work."

"Roger that, Doc. I'm ready."

Immediately, the room became quiet and strangely calm. The monitor hummed softly, and I felt only a slight tug, as the catheter was inserted in my groin. In a few moments, I believe that it was Dr. Eckhardt that said, "Don't move, don't breathe." I did as instructed, and heard a small click on the monitor, as an image was recorded, and the level in my spine noted. I was instructed to relax and breathe again, and the entire process was repeated many times, during the two- hour procedure, as physicians worked meticulously through each level of my spine. Periodically, Dr. Gailloud would ask how I was doing, and, each time, I attempted to reassure him that I was fine. Around the T-10 level, I was aware that more care and time was taken to note all of the pertinent information. While I was unusually relaxed and still, perhaps a result of the mild sedative, I felt almost hyper alert, cognitively, as I tried to ascertain all that was being said. Too much medical lingo for me, though I knew that more was being discussed, relative to the level of my injury. Finally, the tedious and delicate process was complete.

"Pat, you did great. We are done. Give us a few minutes, and we will get you back to recovery shortly. Dr. Orzu and I will come to discuss every-thing with you. Really, you did great. You can be on my team anytime."

"Oh, I want the Heisman, Doc, if I have to play."

Dr. Gailloud smiled again, as he left the room, and I was whisked back to the recovery area, where I was happy to see Raenell coming in to meet me.

"Well," she said, smiling, "I got some Hopkins sweatshirts. I just love this place!"

We chatted about the procedure and what had happened to me with the attending nurse, who indicated that what I had was extremely rare. She helped me sit up and propped a few pillows behind my back and head, as she explained further.

"It's like a surfer's stroke or myelopathy," she explained, "Only yours didn't happen exactly that way. In Hawaii, there have been a few recorded cases of healthy, young people, you know, in the approximately 15-40 age bracket, that have, after they hyper-extended their backs jumping up on their boards, experienced the exact same

symptoms and paralysis as you have reported, when you lifted your garage door. Similar levels in their spines, too. Since 2004, I believe, there have only been 9 or 10 reported cases."

"You mean in Hawaii, alone? What about in other states or countries?" Raenell asked.

"No," the nurse said slowly. "I mean in the world. Like I said, the phenomenon is quite rare."

Silence. No one said anything for a moment.

"Well, damn. I guess I should have played the lottery, huh?" I was having a hard time assimilating all that I had just heard. "That rare, really?" This was not the fifteen minutes of fame I had ever imagined.

"Yes," the nurse continued, "although it is suspected that it may be under-reported, as some of those cases have resulted in recovery, or partial recovery."

I thought about the cases where there must have been no recovery to date, as her statement implied as much, but she had quickly wished me luck, said goodbye, and disappeared down the hall. Dr. Gailloud, along with Dr. Orzu came into the room, only minutes after she had made her exit. I took a deep breath, and silently vowed to hear this news, whatever it was, and face down the fear that was lurking behind every thought. I said I would trust God to help me, no matter what. So now, I had to act on that trust. I tried to smile, but could find no playful words to say. It had all come down to this moment, and I could only ner-vously massage my hands, and wait patiently.

"Well," Dr. Gailloud began, "Pat, I am happy to say that I think we have the best possible news for you, given this whole strange scenario." He paused for only a moment before continuing. "After careful examination of your spinal angio-gram, it seems that all of your blood vessels are now functioning as they should. There are no fis-tulas, malformations, or anything that requires reparation. That part is the best possible news."

"It is?" I felt my chest rise and fall instinctively. "So what does this mean, now?"

"That is the good news – that there is now no obvious venous issue that is contributing to your condition. What you do have, of course, is severe nerve damage, as a result of the initial cessa-tion of blood supply to your lower extremities. As

you may know, peripheral nerve regeneration is excruciatingly slow, and any recovery depends largely on the extent of the damage done, and the ability of those nerves to regenerate. As to whether you will ever walk again, here is what I can tell you. We are not God; therefore, we cannot tell you for sure if you will walk again, or no, or how long that might take to happen. I can tell you that it will be years, not months. But, we cannot find any reason why you might not walk again, either. It is indeed the best news we could give you."

This time, the tears also came quickly, as I put a hand to my lips, as if to help the words find their way out. Dr. Gailloud and Dr. Orzu both hugged me warmly. Nice!

"Thank you," I whispered, "and thank you for taking such good care of me. You Swiss guys are ok. You and Roger Federer, anyway."

"Hey, I said I would take care of you, didn't I?" Dr. Gailloud smiled broadly. "You were the best assistant. More tenacious than even Roger, yes? I am very happy for you. So now, you go work as hard as you can at physical therapy. And never

give up, ok? And let us know of your changes in condition. Don't forget, you will likely have a great deal of soreness in the right groin area, and maybe even some scar tissue, where we had that catheter."

"I will definitely do the hard work," I promised, as both doctors shook my hand once more, and went on to deliver their expertise to others.

It is still somewhat humorous to me, thinking back on that day, that I barely remember getting back in the car. The giddiness must have had its own numbing effect, as I was simultaneously exhausted and exhilarated, as well as starving, since I had eaten nothing all day, and it was now late afternoon. Of course, we had to celebrate once more, with a toast of champagne, as well. I would sleep soundly this night, and be ready to travel back home, as the Baltimore leaves were beginning to turn into rich displays of gold, orange, and red. As we drove out of the city Saturday morning, we caught a glimpse of runners participating in the road race, their legs working madly to propel them onward. Perhaps it was another omen, of sorts. At the very least, I, too, had a long journey ahead. I would go back to Health South for continued outpatient rehab with Jill, my physical therapist, and the wonderful staff there, and I would work as much as I could to get better. Hope was restored, yet again, and I was beyond grateful, and madly happy. I was also quite sure the trip home would be filled with more anticipation and fun chatter with Raenell. Of course, it was!

The Dreams

Isaiah 62:4 NASB "It will no longer be said to you, 'Forsaken,' Nor to your land shall it no longer be said, 'Desolate'; But you will be called, 'My Delight is in Her'..."

January 17, 2015; April 16, 2015

*B*eing a counselor, I have always been a proponent of the power of dreams and the subconscious mind in clarifying life issues, and helping the dreamer to formulate meaningful strategies to solve real problems. But I have always been wary of those who claim to have "heard" God actually speak to them, whether it be through coincidence, a magic sign of some sort, or simply* *their word that they had a super encounter with the holy, as if they had received a direct phone call from a heavenly area code. Of course, I am not qualified to speak to the divine experiences of others; nor, more importantly, to the timing or manner in which God chooses to impart his direction to us. With assurance and humble thanksgiving, however, I can now say that I am certain I experienced a measure of amazing and healing grace, via the realm of dreams.*

I had been overwhelmed with the many impending decisions to make, the painfully slow process of trying to heal, the steady stream of bills, and the unrelenting discomfort of paresthesia, which is the extreme and ever present numbness, tingling, and sharp stinging I feel in my glutes, legs, and feet, every waking moment. Thankfully, many of my friends had graciously donated to the fundraiser that I had reluctantly decided to create, and though it was most difficult to step out of my comfort zone and ask for help, it was a position I felt forced to embrace. Thus, I had recently made the choice to purchase a neurostimulator and a recumbent bike to use in my home on a daily basis, rather than pursuing further out-of-state rehab on a time-limited basis. The process of consideration had been grueling, and communication with certain out -of —state health care staff had been frustrating, at best. I had also just qualified for Social Security Disability, and therefore, physical therapy would eventually take place at The South Carolina Vocational Rehabilitation Center. Though I am a strong woman, I felt my resolve crumbling, at times, and I was exhausted from fitful sleep, since I have to manually turn my legs into any desired position throughout the night. But on this night, I would have one of the most intensely profound dreams that I have ever experienced. I knew, upon waking, that it would somehow be a pivotal point for me, but did not realize how meaningful, or revealing, until I conducted some dream research, using just the simple idream app on my phone.

I am driving in my red Miata, and of course, the top is down. The day is fresh, as in early spring; the trees and flowers are lush and green, as if in the wake of a gentle morning rain. Though I am shifting effortlessly through the gears, while navigating the winding road beneath me, there is a long, thickly woven rope tied to my car on one end, and, at the other, a heavy, square-shaped box that drags precariously along the way. Since it will impede my journey, I park in a sloped driveway of a wood gray home, also impeccably landscaped with large, leafy trees and a variety of flowering plants, and untie the rope from my car. Much to my surprise, the box is a case of beer, no specific brand that I remember, with a man's worn, brown leather wallet tucked tightly inside the carrying hold. In an instant, the house – unknown to me before – is suddenly recognized as the home of the owner of the wallet. I climb back into my car, happy to leave all that I had carried where it belonged. And then, I awaken.

Immediately, I know that the dream is both hopeful and important; initially, because, in it, I am able to drive my beloved little red car. But also because, upon waking, there remained such an overwhelming feeling of peace and wonder in the very specific details, that I knew the dream was highly significant. I was compelled to do some dream research to examine the many elements contained therein, in an effort to discern collective meaning. What I discovered, in the final assessment, was comfort and great hope.

Within a dream context, it is obvious that I am on a difficult journey of immense personal importance; that something is hindering my travel toward my desired destination, or goal. As evidenced by the parking of my car, the time is right for action of some kind. Interestingly – and I thought it humorous, as well – beer, that belongs to others, symbolizes the displacement of hope. Perhaps the greatest discovery was the interpretation of the wallet. Surprisingly, the wallet is synonymous with the dreamer's sense of identity, while finding a wallet indicates a relationship in the dreamer's life that is helping to explore and define the dreamer's true identity. The wood house suggests a place of healing and good health.

In retrospect, after contemplation of the dream, in its entirety, I was both humbled and – at least symbolically – brought to my knees, when I realized the ramification of what it all meant in my current situation. When I bought my little red convertible, it was my early retirement present to *myself. Everything about it was sensuous, exhilarating, and fun. That, in fact, was exactly how I felt when driving it, even just to mundane locations, such as a grocery store. How I miss feeling my feet on the pedals, the way the gears shift purposefully in my hand, the gentle breeze that enhances the feeling of connectivity to everything around me. Driving that car was a simple, but fulfilling pleasure, and was a tangible metaphor for all that was successful and good in my world. So, what does this dream mean in my real life situation? How shall I interpret all of this symbolism?*

In the dream, I am driving up a winding and beautiful pastoral road, energetic and happy, and parking my car to jettison the excess baggage. I believe that means that, though the journey is an extremely difficult one, I am steadfast in my attempt to get to both physical and spiritual wholeness, and that a time to utilize plans for recovery, and implement sound decisions, has indeed arrived. Untying the case of beer that is not mine (a symbol of hopelessness), which is deceptively enticing to hold on to, but, in fact, is slowing me down, and leaving it, along with the wallet (a symbol of an identity of despair for my condition), for the owner of the wood home (God) to keep, was the most revealing part of this dream. Stated another way: Holding on to feelings of self-pity and loss of hope would be understandable; yet, those emotions and identity are not who I am, nor are they part of any divine plan for me. It is acceptable, even healthy, to express sadness over that which I have lost – and, it is a huge loss, to be sure. In stark contrast, however, allowing despair and loss of hope to be consuming is not only unhealthy, but also defies everything that I know a loving God has promised. This dream is a reminder that He is abiding in me – His child – and that I can leave hopelessness with Him. I can scream and cry when I need to do so, and express sorrow, as long as I leave the despair and desolation to the One who wants to lead me into life, to remember my identity as one of His chosen. I can choose happiness and peace amidst this tremendous tragedy. And I never, ever have to give up the prayer that wholeness is, and will be, mine. For that, He has promised, as well.

The second dream, occurring in April of 2015, was kind of a quarterly reminder of the first dream, but with a slightly different theme:

I park my little red Miata on the road in front of another gray, wooden house that I have never seen in real life, but, in the dream, it belongs to my long-time friend, Terri, and her husband, Dave. This simple, one-story home sits on a lake, and both the front and back yards, also lush and green, slope gently downward to the water. I face the house and walk around the right side of it, where I stand in the backyard, facing the large windows in the house, as well as a comfortable-looking screened in porch. I call out to Terri, but somehow, I also instinctively know that no one is home. Glancing back at the side of the house where I had just come from, I see a huge, light-gray-colored snake, very large in girth, tangled up in a knot. I am fearful, but not terrified, as I would have normally been in real life. (Perhaps the time I volunteered to be hypnotized, in a seminar designed to teach a simple hypnosis process for managing phobias, had finally paid off?) Thanks, Fred Mau, hypnotist extraordinaire!) Suddenly, the snake darts across the yard, between me and the house, and disappears on the other side, in another yard, somewhere out of sight. I walk rapidly to my car, taking the same route from which I entered, knowing I will come back to visit with Terri and Dave again. I am content. It is time to go on about my day. And then, I awaken.

Most of the elements in this dream were easily discernable. My cherished red car represents the journey that I am currently taking to get back to a place of wholeness. The sloping, but lush green landscape, along with the wood house, indicates that this journey is difficult, but that achieving happiness, and healthiness is possible, though not yet done. In the dream, the house belongs to my friend Terri, who, in real life, is someone with whom I spent many of the happiest and most fun times of my younger days. While I could not go inside of the house – Terri's home–I believe that the desire to see Terri, and knowing that I would see her again, indicates real-life recognition that progress is happening, though the goal has not been attained. The snake was the only brand new element, missing from the first dream. Although snakes have traditionally been interpreted, thanks to Sigmund Freud, as phallic symbols, some of the more common associations are as follows (see idream app):

- *Snakes indicate one is in the process of resolving difficult issues, or in the process of healing.*
- *Snakes often appear in dreams during times of transformation, or transition.*
- *Snakes can be a symbol of an untapped, or unconscious, resource; or, of intuition, or a deep instinctual drive.*

Of a certainty, all of these interpretations fit, within the context of my specific dream, to under-score my journey to physical and spiritual whole-ness, once again. Interestingly, the snake in my dream was exceedingly large, almost as a fanta-sy-type of serpent, which I believe is a reflection of the size and gravity of my real-life situation. Also notable was the presence of the color gray in both dreams. In both the former and latter dreams, the wood houses were both gray. In the latter dream, the snake was also gray. Gray is a neutral color, and in the dream world, can indicate confusion, isolation, uncertainty, or even lifelessness. Without a doubt, there is much uncertainty and confusion in my life right now, surrounding my paralysis, with all of its debilitating symptoms. At times, I have most assuredly felt painful isolation. My legs have, in fact, become metaphors for lifelessness. But the end of both dreams evoked feelings of peacefulness, and the ability to move forward, despite any uncertainty, or negativity. In both dreams, I drive away from despair and difficulty, happily on a more pleasant journey, and continuing to choose peace and hope. This, I believe, is the deeper meaning of both dreams; that healing – in whatever form it may take – is indeed possible.

Will there be more dreams? I sincerely hope so. I feel a measure of sacredness in them, a connection to both the unconscious and the holy. These dreams are both maps and messages, pleas and prayers. I hold them close, and think about them often, with great anticipation. And with thanks.

March 17, 2015 St. Patrick's Day

1 Thessalonians 5:18 NIV "Give thanks in all circumstances; for this is God's will for you in Christ Jesus."

*O*n the eve of my 60th birthday, which is on St. Patrick's Day, in honor of the saint for which I am named, I found myself thinking about one of my favorite books, Larry McMurtry's Lonesome Dove. One of the main characters, Augustus McCray, played exquisitely by Robert Duvall in the television miniseries, is ultimately faced with his own mortality. As he lay dying from blood poisoning, one leg already amputated, he is speaking to his best friend, Woodrow Call, also magnificently portrayed by Tommy Lee Jones. He smiles, and says, 'By God, Woodrow, it's been one hell of a party!'

Up to this point, I had been somewhat melancholy about the prospect of spending this milestone birthday confined to a wheelchair, instead of in Dublin, Ireland, for the St. Patrick's Day parade of a lifetime. Either that, or perhaps in Jamaica, for my first trip to my favorite band's (Gov't Mule) annual Island Exodus, to revel in the sun, tropical beverages, and the stellar vocals of lead singer and guitarist Warren Haynes. Of a certainty, being paralyzed is not how I had planned on spending this milestone birthday, or any part of my life. Bad enough, I had to miss my first trip to Europe. Could I have the tenacity of an Augustus McCray to adhere to all that is good in this life, even in the face of death? What is it that makes some individuals relish life so fiercely, with an ever-present ebullience that seems to overcome inevitable fears, frailties, and loss? While, in stark contrast, others literally lay down to die, lamenting, 'Has it all come down to this?' while reflecting on missed opportunities and misspent time.

I began to think about many of the events, circumstances, and people in my life. Working partly from a technique I use in my counseling work, I mentally listed some regrets through the years, and pondered their meaning on my life today. Divorce, deaths, two scathing betrayals, an ethical dilemma. What have I learned from them? How have they made me a better person now? And yes, what might have happened had those circumstances been different? Interestingly, while regrettable – and painful, if I allow the memories to be prevalent–none have forever impacted my ability to choose happiness and growth, in the long-term. None have kept me from asking for, or granting, forgiveness when it was so desperately needed – and therefore, allowing God to do the miracle of healing and renewal.

Then, I focused largely on a sampling of events, activities, and people in my life that have brought me immense joy and laughter. They trickled to the forefront of my memory quite randomly, in no particular order, and I was enraptured with them: The birth of my children, dying and hiding Easter eggs with them, and watching as they grew into

amazing young women. Dancing as a "Falconette"
in high school and flipping a rifle in the color
guard. Teachers that made me love literature and
bravely tackle math. Making a real difference in
the live of students I counseled. The life-changing
summer I spent during college as a counselor at
Camp Merrie Woode, in North Carolina, with all
of the crazy adventures and enduring friendships.
Ski trips to Snowshoe, West Virginia, and Aspen,
Colorado. Tennis matches, especially the years
of city and league championships and chances
to play for a state championship. Singing and
playing guitar at church; making a music cd with
my good friend, Richard, in which we did both the
lead and backup vocals and played guitar on orig-
inal songs. Appearing as an extra in a big-screen
movie. Fall camping trips to the mountains, filled
with incredible scenery and non-stop merriment.
Family and girls-only beach trips that always ren-
dered us unable to stand because of uncontrollable
laughter and ridiculousness. Biking and walking at
the beach, and feeling the soft, salty breeze in my
face. My grandfather's unconditional love, and his
eyes that danced when he laughed. The recent

days I had been able to spend time sitting with my aging father. The time I slow-danced, in the middle of Time Square at 4:00 A.M., with an incredibly handsome Danish guy that whispered sweetness, as snow began to magically fall, and Christmas lights sparkled. For a certainty, the many special times in my life far outweighed any sadness. Happily, I recounted the memories, and realized that they, too, were blessings in this life; treasures to be taken out and revisited whenever I needed them. And I needed them now. But I also knew that I needed to make more memories; to make every part of my life count. I could not stop now.

So what did I do for my 60th birthday? My daughters gave a wonderful birthday party for me that was attended by friends and family alike. I actually enjoyed being able to help in the preparations, as I love having parties in my home, and entertaining. Everyone wore the requisite green, and frivolous fun abounded. The 60th birthday came and went, without any major tears. I am still here, still thankful for my life, my children, my friends. Still smiling.

Memories and Setback City

2 Corinthians 12:9 "But he said to me, 'My grace is sufficient for you, for my power is made perfect in weakness'. Therefore I will boast all the more gladly about my weakness, so that Christ's power may rest on me."

*T*he memories are legion. Some difficult to recall, some not so much, and some have been tremendously comical in nature. All are important parts of this recovery effort, and so they are integral parts of my life now. Let's see, some of the more memorable ones:

Hilton Head

When tennis friends Cheryl and Pam wanted to make the trip to Hilton Head, South Carolina, to pick up an electric recliner – yes, the one I later got stuck in when it accidentally became unplugged – I decided to accept the invitation, even though it was right after I had gotten home from inpatient rehab. I wanted so badly to get out, to go somewhere, anywhere, just to feel more normal. The chair had belonged to Cheryl's mother, who had recently died, and the family was willing to sell it at a reasonable price. There were some challenges on that trip, such as being able to climb into Cheryl's husband's huge truck, which may as well have been a mountain. Cheryl and Pam had to push and pull me into the massive front seat in a manner in which I am certain must have been hugely entertaining, albeit somewhat pitiful, as well, since I was just beginning to learn how to handle those kinds of endeavors. The trip down to the coast was fun, and the conversation, even more so. I was so happy to be out of the house and feeling a little closer to normal. Would I ever get back to that place?

Upon arriving at our lunch destination, I immediately found a restroom, which took a gargantuan effort to navigate, not just getting my chair inside, but also making the required transfers. Thankfully, there were no major issues encountered, no one banging on the door to get inside, and we then enjoyed a wonderful seafood meal and stunning coastal view. When we made our way back to the truck, it was yet another adventure in paradise to get me out of my chair and up into the thinner air zone of the gigantic truck. We were all giggling like children at our combined efforts to elevate my behind gracefully. Right about then, three women, from somewhere out of state, appeared beside us on the sidewalk. Having been shopping and enjoying the weather-perfect day, they stopped, rather bemused and concerned, and asked if they could help. Of course, the story of my walking demise came about, which brought tears from all of the women. One of them shared that her husband had recently passed away, and she had also needed to get out and about. They were quite genuine in their concern, and wished us all the very best. That would be my first introduction to just how much most people truly want to help, in any way they can.

Halloween

For some reason, Halloween has always been one of my favorite special days. Perhaps it has something to do with fall being my favorite season, I don't know. As a child, there was absolute magic in being able to transform oneself from one being into another. I think the fantasy was part of the enchantment for me. My early childhood took place largely in the 60's, so it was quite common for kids to dress up, take off down the street, collect one bag of loot, do a quick check-in with the parents, empty out the bag of candy, and head out for fresh hunting ground and a second bag of candy. What fun we had, stomping through the neighborhoods at night, laughing with our friends, and loading up on enough candy to keep every dentist in Columbia busy for the remainder of the year.

When my own children were little, our house was the one that always hosted the neighborhood Halloween gathering. Everyone would gather just at twilight, socialize for a few moments, and then the husbands would take all of the kids out, even pulling some in wagons – or was that the cooler of beer? When everyone was ready to return, they would make their way back to the house, where the ladies were chatting over beverages of choice, watching the simmering food, and answering the door for trick-or-treaters. Everyone would eat, and then the kids would pile into the den, with their candy and a Halloween movie, usually, "Hocus Pocus", which they all adored, and the adults would socialize around the fire, or in the kitchen. This is one of my most loved memories.

In October of 2013, eight months before I became paralyzed, I found myself longing for those days once more, as well as wanting to spend some time in the mountains to see the changing leaves. As I had become accustomed to taking off on a quick trip whenever the mood was right, I made last-minute arrangements to have lunch with Gracyn, who was a junior at

Presbyterian College at the time, on the day of October 31st, and then drive on up the road to spend Halloween night in Asheville, North Carolina. The following day, I would drive back to Columbia, via Brevard, North Carolina, see more leaves and gorgeous views, and then make my way home. When I arrived in Asheville, I rode up to the beautiful Grove Park Inn, which was gloriously attired in mums, pumpkins, and festive autumn leaves. There, I sipped on a warm drink in front of a roaring fire in the great hall, and chatted with other jovial guests. We could not help but smile when a group of local children, all decked out in their Halloween costumes, were escorted into the main area of the inn, where staff members lavished them with many treats. It was such an idyllic scene that early evening, when I made the drive to dinner. Little ghosts, witches, clowns, and the like, with parents in tow, were roaming through mountain streets that were adorned in fall finery. It was a perfect night, and I remember being so thrilled that I had made that trip. Had I known the future – that I would be paralyzed eight months later – I would have stayed much longer, and walked until my legs ached. But then, I am so glad I have that wonderful memory now. It sustains me on difficult days. How I would love to make that drive again!

Halloween of 2014, two months after I returned from rehab, found me celebrating at home, though I longed to take the same trip, yet again. Several tennis friends had also come to the house to keep me company, and I was more than grateful for their presence, on this night, especially. We sat in my living room, which is really more like a second den, but closer to the front door, in anticipation of all the ghouls and goblins. Of course, there was wine, and chit-chat about all of the current happenings in the lives of friends we had in common, and events in Columbia. Every now and again, there would be a knock at the door, with the inevitable young visitors, and I would position the bowl of goodies in my lap, so that rolling to the door was easier.

"Trick-or-treat!" they would exclaim, as they eagerly held out bags and buckets for the expected booty. And I would respond, just as enthusiastically.

"Well, now," I surveyed each one, "what do we have here? A vampire, a robot, Cinderella, and you must be Michael Jackson!"

"Yes!" the little boy waved a white-gloved hand at me and beamed.

I loaded them up with tootsie rolls, and assorted varieties of happiness, and sent them on their way, giddy with excitement about the prospects of more candy and fun with their friends. This ritual was repeated, several times, until the last knock at the door. Upon opening, I found a lone little Minion staring up at me, his yellow costume, with the one big eye, almost too big for his tiny body. I surmised him to be no older than kindergarten age, at the most. At the end of my walkway, his young mother stood, holding a flashlight and a bottle of water, and waited patiently for her little man.

"Oh, my goodness, it's one of those cool Minions!" I loudly announced to my friends.

"Uh-huh," the little Minion replied, thrilled with his catch, "and look at all my candy!"

He held his bucket out to me, and I peered in, as if looking for lost treasure.

"Oh, man, would you look at that! You are going to have dessert forever!" I smiled, tossing in more treats, and waving at his mother, who waved back, knowingly.

""Yes, for a hundred million years!" He breathed, excitedly, as he waved goodbye, and walked swiftly back down the walkway toward his mom.

But halfway down the pavement, he stopped suddenly, turned around, and skipped back to me as rapidly and easily as he could, considering the load he was carrying. Reaching deep into his stash of goodies, he pulled out a large Snickers bar, and held it up for me to take, while staring intently at my wheelchair.

"I hope you feel better."

He said it softly, as he gave a tiny little jump, and then scurried back to his mother, who cupped her hand over her mouth, in sweet surprise at the kindness displayed by her offspring.

"You know what, I feel better already!" I shouted to the precious Minion, as I waved goodbye to him and his mother, while trying to hold back the tears.

So, do you feel better, really, or did you just tell that kid that? Do you believe you can get better, or are you still afraid you won't improve, and that's why those tears are threatening to get out? Or are you just sad that you can't walk?"

I smiled at the thought of a child making me question myself so intently. It was true. I did, indeed, feel better. I was far from healed, at least physically. But I was getting better. Happy Halloween!

Wheelchair Acrobatics

One particularly cool and crisp Friday morning, my friend, Julie, and I had made plans to grab breakfast, and run a few errands while we were out and about. I had just unlocked the door for her, when I realized that I had not fed Annie, my black lab. Now, the entrance to my deck has been ever-so-slightly adjusted, as to allow me to roll in and out, with little effort, so that I can perform simple tasks, such as feeding the dog, and watering some of my plants. This would only take a quick second, I had surmised, as I left my phone on the kitchen counter, which is something I never do. The rule is that my phone stays with me, regardless. But the door is open, and Julie will be here any minute, so I eased out onto the deck with food for Annie.

Perhaps this would be a good time to mention the little adjustment that had been made to my chair the day before. My physical therapist had previously noted that I had not only lost weight, making my chair a bit big for me, but that I had to work unusually hard to reach back, excessively, with my arms to make the chair roll.

"Girl, you are going to tear up your rotator cuffs that way!" Barbara had vehemently noted.

Too late, as I had already had surgery on one, thanks to some mayhem encountered with a van door when my children were little, and had mildly torn the other, thanks to past tennis days. Fortunately, for me, they were healed, and my arms had been fairly strong when paralysis occurred. But I digress, back to the story!

So, my wonderful physical therapist had arranged for one of their chair engineer specialists to take a quick look at my wheelchair, to see if anything could be done to relieve the stress on my arms. Without hesitation, he explained that the seat part of the chair could be adjusted, so that the chair was easier to operate, with much less stress on my shoulders. He instructed me to take it for a spin around the therapy room, while using the utmost caution.

"Be careful, now, when you go up ramps, or anything like that, because the center of gravity on your chair has now been altered, and you could quite easily fall out if you are not careful. You might want to put the anti-tippers back on to help prevent that from happening," he was careful to add.

Why would I put the anti-tippers back on, I haven't tipped my chair over yet. I don't need those! They will only get in the way. Besides, I know how to use this thing now.

When I arrived back at the house that afternoon, I was meticulously careful to take my time coming up the ramp to the side door, as it is one of the more obviously steep inclines that I might encounter. I leaned forward, as instructed, and paid close attention to how the chair was rolling.

Yep, no problem with this at all. Could not have been any easier, and my arms are definitely getting stronger! I am a beast with this business, for sure!

So – where was I? – Oh, yeah, feeding the dog. Anyway, I am on my deck, feeding and watering Annie, and the entire procedure is going smoothly. I have not spilled or dropped anything. I toss Miss Annie a dog bone, and get moving back toward the door. Good for me, as I did it all in record time, and if I hurry, I can grab my purse and phone, and I will be sitting on "go" when Julie walks inside. At least, that was the plan. My first mistake was leaving my phone on the counter; thus, breaking my own cardinal rule. However, it was the second mistake that was the more significant problem. In my rush to get back inside, I had forgotten the simple warning about leaning forward in my chair, when going over any kind of bump – even one as tiny as this. As I pushed forward on the wheels to roll my chair over the threshold, my feet suddenly went airborne, as I watched the footboard quickly come up over my head. It happened so fast.

Oh, geez, this is like "the Zipper", that ride at the fair that flips one completely over! And I can't stop it! Oh no!

Bam! A 360- degree flip! Before I had time to be afraid, or even to take any kind of action to stop it from happening, I had landed, quite unceremoniously on the floor of my deck. I quickly assessed the damage. No blood, nothing broken, at least that I could ascertain. That acrobatic move had to rate at least an "8" for technical merit, though artistic interpretation would likely be severely lacking. My pride, however, had taken quite a bruising, as my legs were splayed at awkward angles, and the snappy little fashion-forward skirt I had on, was twisted about my body like a dishrag. Annie crept slowly over and sat beside me. Gazing inquisitively, she cocked her head to one side, as if to say, "Really?" I could not help but smile, as I rubbed her head.

OK, yeah, that was a pretty dumb stunt to do. Julie must be running late, so I will just call her, and… oh, wait. No phone, you idiot, you left it on the counter, because you just knew Julie would be right here. After everything that has happened to you, you should know that "Murphy's Law" is alive and well!

After one or two choice words with myself, I made an attempt to straighten out my skirt, and readjust my necklace and bracelet. Looking on the bright side, I was thankful that I was not hurt, and that the sun was shining. Brightly. And I had no water, save what was in Annie's bowl. I began to wonder what I would do if temperatures rose, and Julie did not show up, and I was left out here all day in the sun.

"I'm having a 'Lord of the Flies' moment," I whispered semi-humorously to Annie, who continued to stare at me, as I held her face close to mine. "What if I'm left out here all day? What if I have to drink from your water bowl? Arrrghhh!"

Thankfully, there was a knock at the door, and I heard it creak open.

"Pat? Pat, where are you?" Julie yelled from around the corner.

"Sitting on the deck!" I shot back. Literally.

"Oh, my gosh! What in the world happened to you? Are you ok?" Julie stared wide-eyed at me, as she knelt down to pick up my chair. After relaying the sordid tale, and assuring her that I was not hurt, we quickly determined that

185

she could not lift me by herself, and I could not get myself into the chair, even though my arm strength had improved greatly. Much to my chagrin, Julie ended up calling Gary, a guy that goes to our church. Of course, there was not much dignity to be had, as he and Julie hoisted me back into the now upright chair. Oh well. Live and learn, right? Needless to say, my phone never leaves my side, any time I am alone, now. A nice little haute couture cross-body-type of brown leather purse that neatly holds my phone is my life-alert!

Nervous Neurologist

Apparently, Julie and I have one of those nitro-and-glycerin kinds of friendships, where bursts of craziness just happen when we get together. I had my second appointment with this neurologist, for which Julie had graciously agreed to drive, so that we could get lunch afterward. We arrived a few minutes early and began our wait, with Julie reading the book that she brought, while I was skimming through a news magazine, and periodically glancing at my phone to keep track of the time. After an hour wait, I started to watch the clock more closely. After another thirty minutes crawled by, I rolled over to ask the receptionist about the wait.

"Oh, he's double booked today," she responded pleasantly, as if that knowledge would make a world of difference.

"It sounds like he will have a very busy day, for sure" I responded as sweetly as I could. "I, too, have other engagements today. Would you please see how much longer it will be? This kind of wait has happened before. Thank you so much."

With that, I eased back to my seat in a waiting room that now had only two other people in it besides Julie and me. Not five minutes later, we were escorted back to a patient room, where we were again told that the wait would be brief. Another forty-five minutes elapsed, as we passed the time talking.

"Geez, where could that doctor be?" I was getting impatient.

"This is crazy," Julie offered. "You know, I swear, I think I saw him earlier, outside this office, talking on his cell phone."

"Outside there, in the alley?" I pointed to the window, high above us, that was facing the outside courtyard area between the downtown buildings.

"Yes, right out there! I'm certain it was him," Julie waved toward the window.

"Well," I smiled mischievously at her, "there's only one way to find out. Can you climb up in that chair, if I hold it still for you? If he's out there now, chatting it up while we've been waiting long enough to need to color our hair, I'm gonna run him down with my chair!"

We both began to giggle incessantly, like misbehaving children, as Julie removed her shoes and climbed up into the small black leather chair. I locked my wheelchair into place and secured the base of her chair with my hands.

"Just our luck, he'll choose now to come in here," Julie said, as she pulled herself up by the window ledge, laughing hysterically.

"Can you see anything?" I asked quickly. "Is he out there?"

It was at that moment that I looked up in time to see the young doctor, arms akimbo, and staring at us with open mouth and eyes that squinted at us in an obvious question. He stared first at Julie, then me, then back to Julie again, shaking his head. We both erupted in laughter.

"Did you see whatever it was you were looking for?" He asked, eyebrows raised in surprise. "What, exactly, are you looking for, anyway?"

More giddy laughter from Julie and me. Boy, was this effort ever a bust!

"Oh, we thought we heard someone out there we knew," I offered up, stealing a sideways glance at Julie, who coughed awkwardly. "I encouraged Julie to do it, you can blame me."

More laughter from us, and from the doctor, who closed the door, and continued to look at us with doubt. But, we had fun, even if the visit took half the day. Sometimes, I just need to laugh.

Driving

Learning to drive with handheld controls, and purchasing an outfitted car, with a lift for my chair, is definitely one of the more prominent memories. Since my Hyundai Santa Fe sat higher off the ground, and did not have sliding doors that were suitable for a lift, I made the decision to trade it in for a Mazda 5, a type of crossover vehicle that was perfectly suited for my needs, with front doors that had an extra wide opening angle, and sliding doors on each side that were conducive to accommodation of a wheelchair lift, once the middle seats were removed. Thanks to my most excellent driving teacher/occupational therapist, Stephanie, who assured me that I had done extremely well in mastering the rock/push handheld driving system, I easily passed the driving test – yes, I had to take the road test in my car!– and was given a handicapped placard, along with a new license that reflected my acquired status as a handicapped driver, with "preferred parking".

My friend Joel had affectionately named my USC garnet-and-black colored wheelchair, "the Patty Wagon". As a result, I decided to call my car, "the covered wagon" – in keeping with the whole "wagon" theme I had going on. My first venture out on my own, involved a trip to Williams Brice Stadium, the home of the University of South Carolina Gamecocks Football Team. I remember sitting in my parked car, staring at the stadium, and crying, partly because I was finally there again, and partly because I had missed the entire 2014 season. My last visit to that stadium had been with my friend Blaire, approximately two months prior to my injury, when we sat in the stands and watched Jadeveon Clowney, Connor Shaw, and other Gamecock standouts partici-pate in the combines. I had driven my sports car, top down of course, and reveled in the beautiful weather that day, as I walked into the stadium. I hope I get to walk in there again, one day.

Holidays

Thanksgiving and Christmas family gather-ings of 2014 were critical points for me. While I cannot attest to what others might have chosen, faced with my circumstances, I wanted – and needed – to embrace the holidays and fill them with the usual family fun in my home. Of course, there were parts and pieces that I knew would be both impractical and hard on my girls or anyone else involved, so I was willing to relinquish some of those, though a bit sad for me to do so. The biggest of these routines was erecting and decorating the Christmas tree, which usually took its place of ceremony in the room that was now being utilized as my bedroom. Knowing that I could do very little of this work, and that a great deal of time and energy was needed to both set up and take down, I made the executive decision to put a string or two of lights on a plant in the dining room, place the presents underneath, and call it a day. There were both autumn and Christmas decorations, to be sure, as I am a fiend for those kinds of festive embellishments. It was a good decision, however, to place limits on how much we could do, as we decided to place more emphasis on the family gathering, and enjoy time together, instead of trying to do everything just for the sake of decorum. Thus, we all contributed to the effort. McKenna exquisitely prepared her first Thanksgiving turkey that was served with ham, oyster dressing, and a host of the traditional culinary trappings. Gracyn and I prepared other items, as did the rest of the family. The Christmas Eve family time involved the customary unwrapping of presents, followed by a fun and casual family oyster roast. Of course, both gatherings entailed jokes, stories, and our traditional merriment.

Setback City

One of the most difficult events of the past year – and I am dealing with it currently – is the tremendous setback involving my right leg and foot. During the early spring of 2015, I was given a foot plate for my wheelchair to help correct the inward rotation of my right leg, as well as a brace to wear on my right ankle and foot that was designed to help correct the foot drop that I was experiencing. While my left foot would flex readily into a walking position, my right foot had the appearance of a ballet dancer's foot, toes pointed, with very little flexion, and the ankle and foot curved into an awkward, more pronated than normal position for me. Eventually, I experienced swelling in my right calf and some bruising and pressure sores on my foot, as a result of the brace being too tight for me. An MRI and an ultrasound revealed a hematoma in my calf, a slight stress fracture in my knee, and a hairline fracture in my heel. It was a frustrating and emotional setback, as I could no longer use a therapy bike, the standing machine, or attempt any kind of weight-bearing exercise involving my right leg. Even after several months of healing, neither of my physical therapists has been able to make much progress with increasing the dorsiflexion in my foot, though there is improvement in the external rotation of my right leg. Work continues, with guidance from a new physiatrist, in the hopes that surgical repair, a last resort, will not be necessary. I will, however, do whatever it takes.

Swimming

There have been several happy moments of – how shall I say, "stepping stones"- in which I recognized improvements. From seeing twitching in leg muscles, slight motion in my left knee, and finally, being able to kick and move my right leg, each little achievement brought sheer joy. Simulated walking in an auto-ambulator was incredible. Finally being able to maintain my quadraped position (on all-fours) on a therapy mat allowed me to feel muscles trying to work. The most spectacularly happy moment happened when I first got into a saltwater pool for physical therapy, during early summer of 2015. After I mastered just being able to get in and out of the lift, which consists of a chair affixed to a crank system, I took great delight in the way the water made me feel normal – and exhilaratingly free from my wheelchair! That is, after I got used to the strangely numb way my legs felt in the water, and the fact that I could not float on my stomach, due to the changing center of gravity in the body, as a result of leg paralysis. Once the adjustments were made, I discovered that I could easily float on my back and propel myself through the water with my arms. Being a water baby since childhood, I accommodated quickly to the pool environment, and only kept the arm rings on for the ten minutes it took to make sure I was not going to sink when I took them off.

Rehab staff had indicated that, because of the effects of gravity in water, I might be able to experience movement that had been undetectable otherwise. How I anticipated that discovery!

My left leg, though not as stiff and tight as my right, had recovered only small bits of movement in the knee, thus far. As I treaded water, I concentrated on just my left leg, and held my breath as I made the effort to bring my left knee to my chest and push it back down again. "Proprioception" is the medical term used to describe the ability to know where all parts of one's body are, in time and space. Many quadraplegics have lost this ability. I have been most fortunate to retain proprioception in my legs, despite the inability to walk. In water, that ability was heightened, so I was keenly aware of both my legs, as I honed in on the effort to move the left one.

Up down, up down…move! C'mon, lefty, help me stay up in the water!

I don't believe I have ever been so singularly focused on a task before. In that moment, nothing else existed except the connection between my brain and my left leg. And then it happened. The motion was all in my thigh, my knee, and a bit in my calf. Muscles tensing and releasing. Movement that I had not felt in over a year. Raising, pushing, water flowing all around. The shout that came from some primal place turned into uncontrollable and joyous sobbing. I put my face in the water and cried harder, kicking as furiously as my leg would allow. Of course, living in the age of cell phones with cameras, a video was quickly made, and I must admit that I shamelessly posted it to facebook, even though that meant the rest of the world could see me, sans makeup, and in my adaptive suit for the pool. Yep, priorities quickly changed, and I gladly and thankfully shared my miracle. If I can do it in the pool, then one fine day, I hope to do it on solid ground. What a day that will be!

Tennis, Revisited

Another landmark for me was being on a tennis court for the first time, since being unable to walk. Having played doubles right up to the day before my injury, I always enjoyed the cama-raderie, the sweat, the teamwork, the socializing after the match, and everything about this game. When my friend Bryan notified me that he had been asked to handle all of the public address needs for the women's SEC championships, and invited me to attend, I knew I had to go, to get over yet another hurdle. Besides, how could I resist a VIP pass, a great parking place at the beautiful courts at USC, and the chance to see some amazing tennis? But the reality was more sobering, as I pulled into my parking spot, and rolled up to the back entrance gate. My thoughts slipped back to the many times I had jumped out of my car, grabbed my tennis bag and racquet, my container of water, and began to put on a game face for some friendly competition. A few players, lean and muscular, in uniformed but stylish tennis skirts, were warming up on the courts that I could readily see. Serves, volleys, baseline shots were all quickly executed with precision, as teammates pumped each other up while preparing for the match. I sat for a minute by the gate before notifying Bryan that I was there.

Go ahead, cry. Get it over with. You can no longer move your feet like that, or feel the court solidly underneath. You are no longer on tennis teams, or enjoying all of that fun. C'mon, let it go. It's ok to be emotional, coming back like this.

Once the tears were quickly dealt with, and the intensity of the moment back in tow, I could enjoy the day, appreciate the quality of play and practice my neuroplasticity moves. That is to say that I could watch the players closely, and concentrate on envisioning my feet executing the same (well, sort of the same!) lateral and up –and- down footwork. The idea behind the science is to promote the strengthening – in my case, regeneration–of those specific neural pathways, just by mentally practicing the moves. The activity proved to be fun and empowering. Besides, how else could I actually play like those young gals, right? Via the VIP pass, I had the pleasure of being able to sit on court level, actually between courts, so it felt as if I were part of the action. The invitation from Bryan was such a nice gesture, and I was thankful for the opportunity to be there. Another giant felled!

Nancy

Perhaps the most therapeutic experience for me was the visit from my good friend, Nancy, whom I had not seen in over fifteen years. We had met in college, during the summer of 1975, while both working as camp counselors at Merrie Woode, in the Cashiers/Sapphire Valley area of North Carolina. She had attended Louisiana State University, was from Louisiana, and is currently living near Baton Rouge today. Since those camp days, we have stayed in touch, even lived together in Columbia, for almost a year, shortly after the camp experience and college graduation. She has two daughters, as I do, so the parallels in our lives have been quite interesting. I was ecstatic when she finalized the plans to come, and anxiously awaited her 11:30 P.M. flight arrival. Since I could not leave my car in the front of the airport, and had the good sense (it happens occasionally!) not to try to navigate the parking garage at night in a wheelchair by myself, I waited patiently in a parking space right beside the main terminal doors. Thankfully, it was pretty quiet and not crowded at all. Nancy was easily recognizable, and we each marveled at how the other looked, after all these years. We took a leisurely ride back through the nightlights of the city, as we made our way back to the house, noting

many of the landmarks that she was able to rec-
ognize. As one might expect, we were awake until
about 3:00 A.M. that night, catching up, vacillating
between laughing and crying, sharing our stories
and sister secrets, a glass of wine, and our faith
and hope for all good things. It was a most mag-
nificent reunion!

After we had at least some semblance of sleep,
the next day found us sitting leisurely on my deck,
sipping our coffee, and exchanging more memo-
ries, while enjoying the coolness of the morning.
It felt like we had picked up right where we left
off, despite the years of not seeing each other.
For the remainder of the day, we drove around
Columbia to see all of the places she remembered
– the State House, the bank where she worked,
the old apartments where we lived – though the
name had changed as well as the buildings–and
an established shabby-chic kind of eating estab-
lishment on Main Street called "Drake's Duck-In".
Each locale brought more stories, more memories,
and twice the laughter. Naturally, we ended the
day with wings and beer at Delaney's Irish Pub,
followed by a day of going through old photos of

camp adventures, our old apartment, and our trip to Cocoa Beach and Disney World on a spring break to visit her cousin. We were howling at some of the memories of camp time, especially, and thankful that we each could remember different details about specific events. Thanks to the wonders of social media, we were even able to share pictures with Cyndi and Tavia, two of the other counselors who had shared in much of the fun, and lived in Texas and Georgia, respectively. We even made tentative plans to meet in the future – with all agreeing that it would be when I could walk, which made me smile even more.

On her last day here, I had agreed to drive Nancy to Rock Hill, South Carolina, just outside of Charlotte, North Carolina. Our plans included eating lunch with my daughter, McKenna, and picking up Nancy's rental car. She would then drive to see a few more friends in Charlotte, prior to making the drive to Kentucky, where there would be a meet up with members of her church for a mission trip. Of course, there was the inevitable hitch that somehow seems to find us both together. As misfortune would have it, there was a huge glitch in the availability of the rental car, and Nancy was told that it would be a few more hours before it was available. We made the decision to go ahead and get me checked in to my hotel, so that I could freshen up for a later dinner with friends Mary Ann and Bruce that lived nearby. McKenna and her boyfriend, Jake, would also be there for dinner, and we had made plans to go to the new Riverfront the next day.

When we arrived at the hotel, the frustration was compounded by the fact that the handicap accessible room reservation was apparently on the third floor, and not the first, as expected.

"I guess that sign that says, 'In case of fire, do not use the elevator' still pertains to me?" I mumbled sarcastically, but smiling. "Maybe I should practice rolling down the stairs backwards right about now? We didn't go over that in physical therapy, yet, don't you know?"

"Girl, this is crazy, why would they have a handicap room anywhere but the first floor?" Nancy offered. "You'll be toasted before you could even get to the stairs!"

Of course, by now we are giggling and acting pretty goofy, as we hauled me and my overnight bag into the room. While the initial glance of the bathroom revealed fairly well appointed handicap accoutrements, the king-sized bed presented a gargantuan challenge, as the gap between the seat of my chair and the top of the mattress was at least a foot and a half. Nancy stared back and forth, from wheelchair to bed.

"How you gonna haul your behind onto THAT?" Nancy looked horrified. "You need a damn step ladder to get up there! Oh wait – that wouldn't work, either!"

More laughter from both of us. I was not up to the hassle of changing rooms, but knew we had to do something to make it work. My normal transfer would simply require a lean forward and a lifting, pushing and sliding motion that would help me ease my bottom across to my new position, and then placing my legs into position on the bed.

"Well, now, we're just gonna have to get creative here, with the interior décor," I coughed out, as we both continued laughing wildly. "Hand me

that sheet-looking thing that's laying across the bottom of the bed. Ok, now pull that end table, there, right up against the opposite side of the bed from me, and pull one end of this sheet thing around the leg of the table that is closest to the bed. Now hand me both ends of the sheet. Let's see if all those arm exercises I've been doing will pay off, without breaking the furniture."

Nancy did as instructed, while I positioned my chair parallel and flush against the bed and pushed the right handle out of the way. Hoisting both legs, first one, then the other, up and across the bed, I laid them there, while remaining seated in my chair. Next, I grabbed both ends of the sheet that Nancy had arranged for me, and tugged hard on them, as I rolled my body up and onto the bed. We dissolved into fits of laughter yet again, as I lay somewhat awkwardly, but solidly, on the bed. Nancy looked at me, for only the slightest moment, with a visible emotion that was some-where between admiration and pity, and the room grew instantly silent.

"I just don't even know what to say, Pat. How do you do this every day? This is so ..." Her voice trailed off.

"You know me!" I quipped, patting the bed and ready to bring back the levity. "If you ain't living on the edge, you ain't got a view! I have a great vantage point of my room, now that I'm up here on Mt. Everest!

I was trying to keep things light and knew that it was almost time for the hotel shuttle that would take her to back to the rental car, and out of my life for at least a few years. I was sad enough to cry, and was trying hard not to do so. Her visit had transported me back in time, to a happy, safe place, and I realized how much the visit and her friendship meant, despite the years and the distance between us.

"Well, girl," Nancy came to my side of the bed and hugged me tightly. "At least I can reach you from here, without hurting my back," she joked. "I guess this is it, huh?"

I returned the hug just as affectionately. How great it was that she had made the trip, and allowed each of us to fill in the spaces left by the years we spent raising our families and growing into middle age.

"Nan, I can't tell you what your visit has meant to me," I tried to hold back tears, as did she, but we just could not keep them at bay. "Thank you so much – it has meant more to me than you know. We have to do this again."

"We will," Nancy promised, as she made her way to the door, "and we will walk together, you and I. And until then, there's always texting and skype, you know!"

We waved through the tears, and she was out the door. I laid on the bed for awhile and thought about how far I had actually come, despite the big setback. I made a mental note of our promise to take that crazy walk together, somewhere in the future. Guess I'd better get busy, starting with getting ready for dinner. I had also not seen Bruce and Mary Ann in quite some time, and I was grateful to have plans with them, along with daughter McKenna. For sure, taking out-of- town trips were challenging, but fun, so far.

The One-Year Anniversary

On June 28, 2015 – the one year anniversary date – I had promised myself that I would re-read all of the cards and letters I received when this whole ordeal began, and read them every year, until I had either recovered physically, or left this earth, whichever came first. There were way over a hundred of them. No matter. They were each read with great care and placed back into the designated carrying bag. Why, one might ask, would I do that? The simple answer is because that is what I had promised I would do. The more important reason, however, was because that was what I needed to do. It was those encouraging words from friends, near and far, that had helped to carry me through those initial nightmarish days, and I knew, even then, that they would help at all points in this unexpected, devastating, and challenging journey. Somehow, I felt a responsibility to those who had placed so much faith in me to get better. It was a promise I was more than willing to keep.

As a counselor, I have long been aware of how a traumatic anniversary date can impact an individual. On a personal level, I had never been faced with one such as this. After all, there had been no violent, frightening act that had immediately precipitated my inability to walk. One moment I was weak, but walking, and, within minutes, I was sitting on the floor, unable to move my legs. While I remember methodically assessing myself for signs of stroke, or anything else that might possibly present with the symptoms at the time, I also remember simply sitting on the floor for a few moments, as if waiting briefly would make everything alright. Clearly, I had no idea, at the time, of the severity of the situation. No tears, no terror, at least not then. But, as the anniversary date inched closer, I felt the most annoying flashes of fright beginning to appear, somewhere in the back of my mind. By the time that the date was less than a week away, I was almost in full panic attack mode, and, as if that were not bad enough, I had begun to stockpile anger at myself on top of the mounting fear.

"What the hell, this is ridiculous," I remember telling myself. "Why are you fearful now, when it is a whole year later? There is nothing to fear now. It's done. Now, you just have to fight like crazy to get better."

It took me until the Friday before to finally stare the date down and look realistically at what was happening in my head. What I figured out was that I was afraid of revisiting the horror, the memories of all that I had been forced to face in those early days, post injury. Then, I did not know to be afraid, or that anything was terribly wrong. I had been a bit in shock, almost numb, until later that day in the hospital. But now, I remembered every awful moment of facing paralysis, rehab, the unknown of spending a lifetime in a wheelchair, of that indescribably sad night entrapped in the bathroom at Health South. Even though I had made progress over the year in every way, I had not been able to shake the mounting reluctance to deal with the unavoidable that came at me like a juggernaut. Was this what people really went through? Was this anything like what *post-traumatic stress felt like? I felt as if I were trying to crawl out of my own skin, with nowhere else to go.*

On Sunday, June 28, 2015, which was the actual anniversary date, I was supposed to sing and play my guitar in the contemporary service that was held in my church once each month. There was no way I could possibly go to church that day. I believed I would fall completely apart and cry uncontrollably. Worse, I would not be able to get myself out of the front of the sanctuary without help. How embarrassing would that be? When I knew I could not put those feelings off any longer, I sent a message to our organist and choir director, Laura, and told her why I was not sure I could be there. I agreed to come to the rehearsal, always on the Wednesday before the service, and get familiar with the music anyway. Of course, she assured me that it was ok if I cried, which I knew she would say, but this fear was something different. When I opened the binder of prepared music, there was a note from Laura inside. It was a quote from the Gospel of Mark, that simply said, "Fear not. Just believe." As luck would have it, the scripture would be a prominent part of the service. Laura is a master at selecting the most appropriate music to enhance the meaningfulness of every service. As rehearsal progressed, I began to feel an odd sense of relief. What was going on? It could not possibly be this simple. Of course it was not yet June 28, either.

When I got home, I ate dinner and thought about those words again. They were strangely comforting, and a tiny portion of the overwhelming fear had begun to subside.

Fear not. Just believe. Fear not. Just believe.

I looked up the account in Mark: 5. It was the story of the synagogue official, whose daughter was dying, that approached Jesus to ask for healing for his child. Though the man had been told, by others, that she was already dead, he had approached Jesus anyway, and Jesus had responded by telling the man not to be afraid, but just to believe. How did this apply to me? Was I the man in this story, or the little girl? Either or neither? Did it matter? And then it hit me, dead on. I was both. Fear was slowly killing me. If I let it continue, I would be dead, like the young girl, at least spiritually. Like the man, I wanted help. I wanted to no longer fear. But, how to get rid of it before it became more overpowering?

Fear not. Just believe. Fear not. Just believe. So, how do I "just believe" I'm not going to be a basket case on Sunday, when the fear is almost debilitating now?

I sat quietly for several more minutes, chewing on the words. It seemed so trite, so condescending, as if someone were patting me on the head and ignoring my feelings. And then that inner voice somewhere, that spoke so softly.

"I know your feelings. You are afraid, really afraid to relive that awful day, as well as the days that followed. I am here. I'm listening. Didn't I say I would never leave you, no matter what? Where is your faith?"

My faith. That was it. I had momentarily lost my focus; allowed my thoughts to drift to those of worry and deep fear, instead of holding on to promises from a loving God that had been made to me. It was fine to acknowledge my fear and my weakness in handling it, and I had done just that when I shared those feelings with Laura. I had also made the decision to go to rehearsal anyway – a step toward reclaiming that bit of faith in which I had let go, albeit somewhat unwittingly. That was why I had felt better. But now it was, quite literally, time to meet the music! I had to make a conscious decision to place my trust, my faith with God. Would I be a mess on Sunday? Maybe. If I sit home and think about it, or go for a nice drive somewhere and cry it out, I will be a mess, regardless. I sent Laura a note and told her I would sing and play on Sunday.

Saturday evening, June 27, I showered and waited until about 10:00 P.M. to pull out the cargo bag that contained all of the treasured messages of hope. I read every single one; slowly, carefully, and thought about the sentiment conveyed in each. Of course, there were tears. The expressions were heartfelt, and I took a long, hard look at just how far I had come, though knowing I had yet an eternity to go. This time, the tears were not of fear; rather, they were from the assurance I took in knowing that I was so loved and cared for. When I finally finished, in the quietness of the wee hours, I was tired in the most satisfying of ways. I would sleep solidly through the night, past those terrible moments of 5:30 A.M., and wake up refreshed and ready to enjoy the service of worship. It was a magnificent service, too, if I do say so, myself! The music was particularly glorious and clear, and I felt stronger than I had in days. How glad I was that I had taken yet another victory in my recovery!

"I told you so." That soft voice whispered.

"And, as usual, You were right." I said out loud.

A Comic Interlude, Take Two (More Wheelchair Tips and Quips)

Luke 6:21 "...Blessed are you that weep now, for you shall laugh."

1. *Be careful when in a wheelchair and rolling past an open refrigerator. The small trays in the door love to jump out and attach themselves to various parts of the wheelchair. And the bottles of salad dressing, mustard, ketchup, and soy sauce manage to come with them.*
2. *"Don't worry, I brought my own chair," is a great party-starter, when in a wheelchair at a crowded restaurant table.*

3. *Lights that are on a timer system can be very challenging, when alone in a wheelchair in a public bathroom. In a stall. With no windows.*

4. *An electric recliner is a wonderful invention. Unless it becomes unplugged while one is lying in it, out of reach of the plug. Paralyzed. And home alone.*

5. *There are rain ponchos big enough to cover a wheelchair and its occupant. Color is important here. Fluorescent orange creates the illusion of The Great Pumpkin on wheels, and is highly entertaining. And very visible in parking lots. Not altogether a bad thing.*

6. *Having one's favorite Chinese take-out haunt on speed-dial is very helpful, when paralyzed. Having the sweet little Chinese woman who works there willing to bring one's food to the car, is even better. Unless she's not there one day, and one must deal with a male employee, who appears to speak little English, at least on the phone. Coincidentally, the fortune*

cookie said, "Communication is key in the best relationships."

7. *Having an extra set of house keys in one's purse, when outside, is a good idea, in case the first is dropped somewhere not easily retrievable from a wheelchair. Not that this would actually occur.*

8. *Sweeping the floor can be rather challenging in a wheelchair. An acquired skill. Time-consuming, too. But rewarding, in a bizarre kind of way.*

9. *Seeing one of those insidious little cockroaches, or "palmetto bugs" is bad enough, when one can walk and actually go after them. It's a bit more unsettling when one has to chase them around, while in a wheelchair. Bug spray can only reach so far!*

10. *Smoke alarms are great to have mounted on the ceiling. Unless the batteries die. Late at night, when no one else is around. And one is in a wheelchair. Could cause some serious head-banging.*

The Interviews

Ephesians 4:15   "Instead, speaking the truth in love, we will grow..."

Pat, what has been the hardest part of this whole experience for you?

*H*onestly, the loss of good mobility, of independence in being able to go and do even the simplest of things, like helping my father, who is now 90. The setback of having to try to correct my right leg and foot has been very frustrating, because I'm ready to get things done, and this setback is not on my timetable, you know! I also hate having to ask others to help me. That has been a lesson in humility. As shallow as this may sound, not being able to drive my little red car has been a huge stumbling block for me. I guess that car is kind of a metaphor for where I saw myself in life – an "older model, but still a classic, still happily on the go". I so miss my spontaneous trips, being able to dance, go upstairs in my own house, walk on the beach, or even carry all of my own groceries to my car. I long for those kinds of simple things. Also, knowing how much my paralysis has impacted my girls, and it has impacted them very differently, I think. For instance, McKenna wants to do this interview, but Gracyn does not. She feels, rather emphatically, that this is "my story" to tell. I want to respect the feelings of both my girls, and need to honor both of their choices, so that's ok. McKenna and I wanted to do this, so we all agreed that this is how we would handle it.

Do you ever feel physical pain in your legs? Can you feel them now?

Are you kidding? Yeah, it's pretty frustrating, sometimes. The paresthesia – the tingling, burning sensation due to both nerve damage, and possibly nerve regeneration – is an ever-present reality, a constant. By that, I mean I feel it in my glutes, and in my legs, all the time. Unless I'm asleep. It can wake me up, at times. I absolutely despise taking medicine for anything, but if I don't take the gabapentin to diminish the neuropathy, the discomfort can become intense, and feel like the top layers of skin have been burned off. I have a pretty decent tolerance for pain, so I'm doing well to take a minimal dosage, but I freely admit that I have to have it, or I could not deal with the level of pain that can happen. At least, with the medicine, it feels like everything is asleep. Ok, asleep, times ten, if you can imagine. Neurostimulation helps, too, and seems to be warding off the muscle atrophy, to a good extent. And I do think that the neurostimulation may be encouraging the nerves to regenerate, at least I hope that is the case. Swimming has helped, also, with regard to pain management. And there's always alcohol. OK, yeah, I'm kidding about that. I'm really not a big drinker, as much as I tease about it. The truth is, an occasional glass of something every once in a while is nice, but I can actually go weeks without it, as well. Alcohol, if overdone, can also interfere with medicine, so I always take good care not to diminish the effects of that which helps me!

What advice would you give to others who might find themselves suddenly paralyzed, or handicapped in such a manner?

It is critical that one not give up hope. Never give up trying to get better. There are some, even doctors, that will say your condition isn't ever going to improve. Do not listen, and do not ever give up. That does not mean that one blindly ignores reality. But the truth is, every condition, every person, is different. There is healing power in not giving up. Let prayer requests and hard work become routine, no matter what anyone else says. Be a realistic advocate for oneself. Read up on whatever the condition might be, ask many questions, get a second opinion. Unfortunately, there is not much research out there for my specific condition, because it is so rare. But looking for clinical trials, and staying in touch with my doctor, Dr. Leslie Stuck, has been critical. Find a caring physician! She sees me once every three months, and that has been tremendously helpful and supportive. For me, staying in touch with friends, with my church, and keeping active as much as I can, has also been hugely important. When learning to navigate with adaptive devices, such as a wheelchair or an adapted car, sometimes practice and trial and error will be the best teachers. Accept the tears. They will come and go, many times. Have I mentioned prayer and hard work–again? A little laughter won't hurt, either. Listen to good music. Get up everyday. Be thankful, no matter what. Oh – physical therapists are incredible people. They can be powerful allies and advocates, too. I have been most fortunate to work with good ones, Jill and Barbara, and my case management person, Ella, has been incredible, as well. Each professional is different, too. No one person has all the answers.

McKenna, how did you feel when you found out your mom would be in a wheelchair?

I don't remember a specific moment that I knew she would be in a wheelchair. We took each bit of news as it came, one day at a time. Gradually, the long-term reality began to sink in with every challenge. I've had moments when it really hits me and I feel unsure or sad for the future. While backpacking one weekend with friends, we passed a young couple hiking with their baby and parents. My friends joked about how their parents would never do something like that because it wasn't their thing. I quietly wondered if my mom would ever be able to consider an active life with me again. Despite the uncertainty and long road ahead, my mom has remained incredibly tenacious and positive. I still have a feeling in my gut that she will recover... it will just take a little more time and patience than we thought. I am thankful every day that she is not fighting for her life, and has the hope of walking again, for motivation, which is something many people fighting a life-threatening disease, or accepting the aftermath of a tragic accident, do not have.

How has your mom's condition impacted your life?

It's made me appreciate my mobility. I feel a stronger obligation to live actively and travel as often as possible, since she cannot. Right before my mom's paralysis, I planned a trip to the northwest since I considered moving to Seattle. I was excited about living more on my own and focusing on my career. I knew it would be difficult leaving my family, to see them only once or twice a year. I considered the chance of something happening to my mom or dad. They are divorced and do not have a significant other, so I feel that my sister and I are even more responsible for their well being if anything happens. But they were both healthy and active individuals, so we didn't have anything to worry about. A week before I flew out, mom was in the hospital. It didn't feel right leaving her or my family while this was going on. It all worked out, though. South Carolina feels even more like the place I need to be in right now. I wouldn't want to miss my mom's first steps, if she regains the use of her legs.

What has been the hardest thing for you, in all of this?

It's really tough seeing her in this condition and how it's changed her body. Naturally, I wonder if it will be permanent. I worry about the way the paralysis has caused her right leg to stick out some, and her ankle to curve in, if that will impact her ability to walk, if she gets to that point. At times, I struggle to stay positive for her, to hide any doubts, or not burst into tears when she has an emotional breakdown. Sometimes I feel a disconnect from the reality of the situation. Maybe it's the result of a defense mechanism to avoid any amount of grief or guilt. I live out of town while her friends and my sister are there most often. Mom has been paralyzed for over a year now, but every time I come home it's like the coping process starts over, in a different way. On Sunday, I drive back to where I live and her condition is out of sight until the next time I visit, and a new challenge is presented.

Another difficulty is determining how to appropriately be there for my mom in a way that is supportive, while staying true to developing a life of my own. My mom has spent the better part of twenty-five years keeping my sister and I in place, teaching us to be independent, and caring for us when we could not do it alone. She did a damn good job raising us, but to a mom, that job is never over. It must be very difficult for her when the role of a mother and child feels reversed. In the beginning, I watched her hold on to any bit of normalcy and make solo decisions to feel in control of her situation. Nobody wants to be a burden—my mom is not one—but in order to get on with a new way of life, sometimes, she has to rely on the help of others. Mom isn't figuring this out alone.

The Thousand Year Flood

Psalm 69:2 "I sink in the miry depths, where there is no foothold. I have come into the deep waters; the floods engulf me."

There are two old sayings, here in the Deep South, when a person plans to act on good intentions. It might sound something like this:

"Liza, you coming to the reunion on Sunday?"

"Yes, I'll be there, God willin', and the creek don't rise."

-Or-

"Yes, I'll be there, come hell or high water!"

But on Sunday, October 4, 2015, the creeks, rivers, and canal did indeed rise, and there was hell and a lot of high water in Columbia, South

Carolina. Off the Atlantic Coast, Hurricane Joaquin was churning madly, at Category 4 status, with winds over 150 mph, while a low-pressure weather system hovered over the Carolinas and Georgia, pulling in even more moisture, and dumping historic amounts of rain on Columbia, and particularly in our Forest Acres area of town. It would be the perfect storm, a flood that would only occur once in a millennium. Most of the rain had been initially predicted to happen Saturday, the day before. When that did not occur, the rains that started in the pre-dawn hours on Sunday morning would end in torrential flooding and life-threatening scenarios for many.

At 5:00 A.M. on Monday morning, my father, who is 90, and his wife were awakened to find that their home had two feet of water in it, and the water level was rising rapidly. Neighbors quickly rushed in to help, with three men who pushed Dad out of the driveway, in his wheelchair, through what was now chest-deep and freezing cold water, and up the hill to safety. Many in Forest Acres had to be evacuated by boat, leaving all of their belongings, and life as they knew it, behind. Suddenly, I was terrified of what could happen to me, being in a wheelchair. Could I get stuck like my father had in rising waters, and not be able to get to safety? The death toll was mounting; fifteen would eventually lose their lives. What if it were my car that had fallen into a black hole in a road? Even if I could out of a car – which was doubtful – I certainly could never get myself out of muddy hole filled with rising water. The flood became real and more frightening than I could imagine. I had lost my foothold to fear, to panic, to the reality that my paralysis now presented. I felt more vulnerable than I ever had before.

My friend, Kat, had come to stay for Saturday night only, but upon waking Sunday morning, she decided to stay another night. It quickly became obvious that she would not be able to go home anytime soon. The pond in my backyard was rising rapidly, with water flowing, unimpeded like a river, and down to neighbors in the lower sections of the watershed. For the next two days, we watched TV news reports, anxiously awaiting all of the updates about power outages and evacuations. Somehow, my house had been spared, as we still had power and water. We remained motionless in front of the TV, reluctant to believe all of the destruction and despair we were witnessing. However, when the alert came for the entire city, in which all were instructed to boil water before using, we went into action immediately. Large pots, as well as a party -size electric hot beverage urn, were activated, and before the day was done, an admirable supply of water had been boiled and placed in usable containers. We kept our phones and my computer powered up, also. My friend Alicia had been to the store for me, and Kat had gone, as well, so we were amply supplied with necessities. Of course, being the candle freak that I am, those were around in bulk, and we lit several, while awake, in anticipation of losing power. Thankfully, that never happened.

By Wednesday morning, it was clear that this flood had been a record-breaking, phenomenal catastrophe, by all accounts. Many of the national weather celebrities were covering the flood disaster here, and commenting on how well our little state had handled all of the adversity thrown at us recently. From the shooting of the Mother Emanuel parishioners in Charleston, and the resulting decision from the governor that would end with the very public removal of the Confederate battle flag, to the shooting of a young Forest Acres police officer, our city and state had weathered much. And now, the weather itself was dealing the third strike. Before I had gotten out of bed, a loud, shrill alarm emanated from my cell phone, urging residents in my area to get to higher ground, immediately.

I got into my wheelchair as quickly as I could, turned on the TV, and called Kat, who was in an upstairs bedroom.

"Yeah?" she said sleepily.

"Kat, get up, we have to go now. We have been told to evacuate. The Windsor Lake Dam is getting ready to break, and it will flood this area."

"What? Ok, ok, I'm on the way!"

Due to the slightly obsessive part of my per-sonality – the latent girl scout that was always prepared–I had slept with my clothes and tennis shoes on, just in case. Grabbing my overnight bag, already with a few items inside, I began tossing in the other essentials, then rolled quickly into my bathroom and reached for my bag of toiletries. My morning routine would have to wait.

Think! What else? Medicine for neuropathy, valuable information?

Kat was soon down the stairs, belongings in hand, and ready to go. The night before, we had discussed an evacuation plan, should one be necessary. She had wanted me to go with her to the home she shared with her husband that was a good thirty minutes away. I had not wanted to go, as there were stairs to negotiate and no handicap accessibility. We had agreed that I would go to my friends, Ginger and Gary's home, which had a ramp and other necessities to accommodate a wheelchair, and she would go to her home. The prior decisions had given us extra time to be as ready to leave the house as possible, so we were out of the door promptly and heading down the ramp, when a black truck came around the corner and swung into my driveway behind my car. It was another close friend, Aubrey, who was the father of one of my oldest daughter's friends. He jumped out of the car and gave the command for the chocolate colored dog in passenger side of the truck, to stay there.

"Pat," he blurted out with concern in his voice, "I was out early this morning, and Hallie called to tell me about the evacuation in your area. I came as soon as I could! What can I do?"

"Aubrey, my dog, can you get her for me, while I get myself in my car? Annie, she's in the back yard!"

Aubrey stood beside my car, as I hoisted myself up onto the board that folded down from the driver's seat. Kat was quickly shoving my bag into the back seat, behind where my wheelchair would be, and tossed my other bag into the rear of the car.

"Pat, I can take Annie with me. She will be fine at our house, ok? What else do you need?" he looked at me quizzically.

"I need the papers, all of my important papers, with insurance information, and all. Can you go in the house and grab those?"

I gave him instructions to find the papers in a specific file cabinet. Instantly, he and Kat hurried back into the house and were back out as I was setting myself into the driver's seat and plugging my phone in. Aubrey was carrying the entire file cabinet down the ramp, and Kat was locking the door.

"Ok, sweetie, we will take care of everything, don't you worry," he smiled, as the file cabinet and Annie were quickly lifted into the back of his truck. "You just call us when this is done, and we will get Annie and the cabinet back for you."

I looked at Aubrey, then at Kat, who was already in her own truck, and waiting on me. I stared at my house. Would it be there when I got back? The pictures on the wall, my guitar, all of the sweet notes my children had written over the years? I might not see any of it again. What would I do, then? I could feel the tears trying to get out, but I refused to let them, at least not yet.

"I can't thank you enough, Aubrey. Please tell Barbie and Hallie that I'm thinking about them, as well. I guess I should go, now."

With that, Aubrey disappeared around the corner, and Kat followed me down the street and around the convoluted route we were forced to take because of the roads that had been compromised by caving holes and flooding water. When we got to Two Notch Road, where I would go left, and Kat, right, we waved frantically to each other and went our chosen ways. I took in the scene around me. Detoured traffic, holes in roads, bright orange barricades, helicopters over- head, and an array of police, firemen, and other first responders that buzzed incessantly amidst it all. I felt small – even more handicapped–in my car, with my wheelchair. The feeling of helpless- ness permeated my every thought.

"Lord, please just let me make it to Ginger's house" I prayed silently to myself, as I drove down Two Notch Road.

I think I prayed, in some manner, all the way to Ginger's house. When I arrived, Ginger appeared in her driveway, and husband Gary followed shortly thereafter, to give me the news that the Windsor Dam had, in fact, not breached, and that the evacuation order for my area had been lifted. What a relief it was to hear that news! However, I was keenly aware that circumstances could change at any moment. I visited with my friends in their driveway, fueling up on reservoirs of relief and moments of calm, before I made the decision to return to my house. My home had been spared, and my family – despite the scare with my father –was safe. There was much to be thankful for on this day. As I eased up the ramp in my garage, I stopped to touch my little red Miata, and could not help but shed a few tears.

"We're still here," I whispered, "and we are both ok! We have survived much, you and I. I wonder what the future holds for us?"

Pat, you are talking to a car. A car! Get a grip.

Yep, it could be true – that which does not kill us, does indeed make us stronger. Maybe crazier, too. I had to smile.

On Saturday, October 10, 2015, the USC Gamecocks were scheduled to play LSU here in Columbia at Williams-Brice Stadium. With roads severely damaged and compromised by flood waters, a city-wide boil water alert still in effect, with first responders and law enforcement that were already stretched to the limit, the prudent decision was made to play the game in Baton Rouge. Having experienced the same kind of trauma during Hurricane Katrina, LSU acted quickly and positively to make what was supposed to be a home game for USC into a positive visit at LSU, instead. Roundtrip flights, hotels, welcome billboards, meals for the team and many fans were all arranged. The LSU band expertly played our pre-game "2001" and fight song, as well as our alma mater. They clapped, cheered, and did everything possible to make the visiting Gamecocks feel at home in spite of such dire circumstances.

Of course, through all of the days of our flood disaster to the day of the big game, my friend, Nancy, and I had texted back and forth. As usual, she had offered support and love during the toughest parts, as she has done throughout my ordeal, thus far, with paralysis. Finally, a brief reprieve from all of the hard days! How cool it was that our two schools were playing each other in this manner! I was excited to be getting ready to have friends Larry and Elaine, both of my girls, and several of McKenna's friends over to watch, even though our team was not predicted to win. Twenty minutes til kickoff, and I was so ready for some fun.

Wait – here's a text from Nancy now! I began to read.

"Dear friend, hate to break this to you via text, and I wanted to wait until your dangerous, terrible situation was somewhat passed. I'll put it in a nutshell, as I had to digest it a bit myself! I have been diagnosed with lung cancer…"

I tried to read more…left lung, PET scan, chemo, no surgery or radiation…something about God's peaceful presence making it all ok for her and her family…but all I really heard was "cancer". It was bad enough for me to be experiencing such difficulty, but not this. Not my friend, too.

"No!" I raged silently. "Not her! Not her! No! No! No!"

But the horror of this disease was front and center. I covered my mouth with a hand, squeezing hard to keep from screaming out loud, but the tears came, this time violently, and I sobbed, rocking back and forth. Memories of all the fun times bombarded all at once, compressed, and catalogued in my mind. I recalled the death of my mother, who had smoked heavily most of her life, and finally died from this most dreaded illness.

I frantically searched for a reason. I had never even seen or heard of Nancy smoking. Thankfully, McKenna was the only one here at that time, and she came quietly into the room and gave me a hug and soothing words of comfort. I pulled myself together for the company that would be arriving in mere seconds, and texted Nancy back, offering love and a listening ear. We agreed to talk soon, and reminisced about the crazy and fun time we attended an LSU game together, when we were both college students. That trip to Europe that I missed? The reunion with camp buddies? Yeah, we will do those, too, one day. God willin', and the creek don't rise! Come hell, or high water, my friend. We will both be there.

In The Valley, Part Two

Hosea 2:14-15 "Therefore I am now going to allure her; I will lead her into the wilderness and speak tenderly to her. There, I will give her back her vineyards, and will make The Valley of Achor a door of hope. There, she will sing as in the days of her youth…"

John 11:25 "Jesus said to her, 'I am the resurrection and the life. The one who believes in me will live, even though they die'."

Joan of Arc "One life is all we have and we live it as we believe in living it. But to sacrifice what you are and to live without belief, that is a fate more terrible than dying."

The Feast of the Epiphany, on January 6, is a festival day in which Christians celebrate the manifestation of Christ to the Gentiles, as represented by the Magi, or Wise Men. When I was a teen, my church celebrated this day with a Feast of Lights pageant that was always held at dusk, and told the story of the Light of Christ, and how it was, and still is, spread through this world. This was a beautifully meaningful and fun service that deeply engaged the participants in the use of carols, costumes, incense, and candles. Very brief stories were told about biblical characters, such as the apostles, saints, Mary and Joseph, missionaries, the Wise Men, and the like. Many of the youth in the church were asked to be in the pageant and dress as one of the historical people.

When I was about fifteen, I was asked to be in the pageant. I remember excitedly hoping that I would be chosen to be Mary, the mother of Christ. Well, of course, that was another incident of temporary teenage angst with which to reckon, as I was given the role of St. Joan of Arc. No pretty head covering, and gentle gown to wear, proudly holding the baby Jesus, and sitting next to whoever was the likely hunky Joseph that year. Oh no, it was a plain, short brown tunic and black stockings and shirt, and a sword for me.

"Well, I certainly look like a soldier," I thought, as I stared at my image in the mirror.

As I am an avid reader, my father had a pretty good idea of how to shake me out of the doldrums of not getting the assignment I wanted. He quickly suggested a reading on St. Joan, to glean all the information I could about her, so that portraying her might be more interesting. I was even allowed the use of the family car to make the trip to the library for her biography. It would have been so much easier with the internet, but looking back on the whole affair, perhaps the book and time alone with her story was just the remedy I needed. As I thumbed through a biography I had plucked from the shelf, I noted that Joan had been only nineteen years of age when she was burned at the stake in 1431.

"My dad was only 19 in WWII, when he was shot and also captured in France, as she was captured," I noted. "This could be kind of interesting."

And interest turned to fascination, as I had read at least one-fourth of the book before I left the library. It seems that young Joan was a simple farm girl, growing up in medieval France, never learning to read, nor write. In her early teen years, she believed that voices sent from God were telling her to save France from the English, during the time of The Hundred Years War, and to help Prince Charles become King Charles VII, the rightful monarch of France. Prophesy and rumors had abounded that a young maiden would save France from the English. As a mere girl, with no training at all, she convinced Prince Charles of her sincerity and divinely inspired ability to help him. Donning armor and military accoutrements of that time period, Joan was successful in lifting the siege of Orleans; thus, her fame and reputation grew. When finally captured by the English, she was tried for heresy, witchcraft, and "cross-dressing" like a man, and subsequently burned at the stake. It is said that her request was for a crucifix to be held before her eyes, so that she might remain focused on it at her death. Afterward, her fame spread even more. Prince Charles became King Charles VII, and eventually had Joan retried, and found innocent of all charges. In 1920, Pope Benedict XV canonized her, and Joan became St. Joan of Arc, Patron Saint of France.

My adolescent self was hooked. I drove home with a new fascination and respect for the young woman who spoke her way into not only an audience with a prince, but also into an integral part of history. My parents, of course, wanted to know what I had learned, and what I thought.

"You were right," I admitted, as I delivered a somewhat rebellious and well-crafted, "I love her, she's bad-ass!"

Naturally, I got the expected responses, along the lines of "Patty! Young ladies don't talk like that!" But, I also knew that, given the circumstances, there would be no consequences for bad language. Parents love to be right. Besides, I saw them smile, just briefly, as I went about the business of being me.

The evening of the Feast of Lights pageant found me dressed in my brown leather tunic, with black tights, shirt, sword and candle. A dull fashion statement, compared to Mary, the Magi, and all the rest. But, I happily made my way down the dimly lit aisle toward the front of the church. As I moved slowly forward in the sanctuary, I heard a distinctly young male voice, just above a whisper.

"Nice legs, Joan," he muttered.

I could not help but grin. After recently being rid of the metal braces that had been on my teeth for the better part of four years, and replacing my horn-rimmed glasses with contact lenses, I was newly into recovering my femininity, instead of looking like a human lightening rod. Yes, I was Joan! Saint Joan, and proud to be so chosen! But, fast forward to today. It is now mid-October, 2015. This time, last year, I was getting ready for the trip to Johns Hopkins Hospital, wondering what had really happened to those legs, to my body. After all, where I am now is a far cry from the young woman that walked proudly that night at church. Though I have recovered some good movement and sensation, and have, by all accounts, made progress, I am still not walking, which remains the elusive goal.

One day at church, as I was rolling out of the service, an elderly woman with a walker, named Janet Martin, approached me. Janet is easily one of the most revered and loved personalities in our parish family. She wanted to remind me of the time that I was selected by her to be Joan of Arc in the Feast of Lights pageant so many years ago.

"You know, I see you fighting so hard to remain positive, and to walk again. When I think of you walking down the aisle that evening back then, I know I was right to pick you to be her. You will always be Joan of Arc to me." She smiled warmly and patted my hand.

I thanked her profusely, with all of the politeness I could muster, and exchanged a few niceties. Then, I made my way, as quickly as I could, to my car. Thankfully, I was able to hoist myself into the front seat, and drive down to a more private area of the parking lot before I broke down, emotionally. I cried because her words were so incredibly thoughtful and inspiring. I cried because I could no longer walk down any aisle, or beach, or shopping mall, or worn earthen path. I cried because there are times when I don't feel so pretty or strong or courageous, or youthful anymore. I cried because I'm nowhere as valiant as Joan of Arc, and I had foolishly not wanted to be her when Janet picked me to represent her place in history. I cried because I had an epiphany of my own.

Whether I ever walk again or no, I can never stop believing that I will. I know I must always try. That belief – that kind of drive – yes, even positive stubbornness, is an essential part of who I am, and I should never ignore that. It is a way that I have chosen to live the one life that I have been given, with or without legs that work. In the meanwhile, I will sometimes cry, amidst the laughter, when I most miss the ability to walk and enjoy the many activities that I can no longer do in the same way. The loss is monumental, to be sure. But such is the nature of life, with difficult trials that, on occasion, test our very ability to live and breathe.

After spending a little over a year with paralysis, I have come to intimately know about life in

The Valley of Achor – both the excruciating agony of pain and desolation, as well as the sweetness of hope and joy in all good things. It would be a lie of gargantuan proportions to say that I do not miss my prior walking life. In truth, I would give any amount of money to have it back. But it is also true that, even when walking again, the experience of paralysis is tattooed forever and deeply in the sinews of my soul. Unquestionably, I am a better person, having experienced the immensity and rawness of human emotion and pain that is the psyche of extreme tragedy. My life has been rearranged in ways that I never thought possible: priorities changed, relationships enhanced, goals solidified. Just as the pain was enhanced, exponentially, so now is the hope. And it is mine forever, for which I am truly thankful.

Mark Twain once said, "Whatever thing men call great, look for it in Joan of Arc, and there, you will find it."

Perhaps the greatest quality about Joan was her faith in God that rose above all of the improbabilities in her life. She lived simply, with great hope, purpose, and passion; a girl light-years beyond her time, looking past her own weakness. Even at the hour of death, she remained fixed on the Christ, her Lord of Life. How I want to live like that, for it is certainly the mark of a life well lived!

Where will my life – my choices–take me, now? The answer is that I do not know for sure. Always, my hope is to walk, to be able to live the remainder of my life with legs that will let me walk through the hills and valleys. Regardless, my life will go on. Right now, the top of the short list plan is to pursue my physical therapy with a vengeance. My legs are so much stronger. I am in this fight for as long as it takes. I once promised an English teacher I would write a novel, and I am way overdue on that particular task. Playing my guitar with much more finesse, which could easily take up several lifetimes, is on that list, as well. Of course, I will remain active in my church, travel as best I can, spend time with my girls, enjoy my friends, and listen for the direction God chooses to send me.

Joan of Arc once said, "Act, and God will act."

In life, one is presented with many choices, and therefore, with many possible consequences.

The only guarantee that came with my choice to believe and trust in a loving God, was that He would always love me, and work for good for me; that He would never leave. Because I have chosen to believe, I must also choose to act; and then, trust God. And you know my philosophy.

If you ain't livin' on the edge, you ain't got a view.

Capta majora.

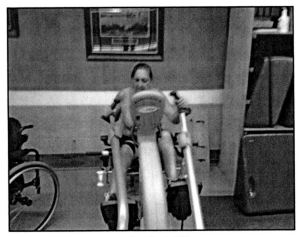

workout at PT

Nancy and Pat

the 60th birthday

the bike

When these legs worked....that's still the
goal and the prayer!

Riptide By The Bay with Raenell

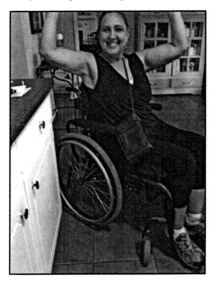

I'm going to be ok!

CPSIA information can be obtained
at www.ICGtesting.com
Printed in the USA
FFOW05n1351021215

9 781498 455961